THE
NO SWEAT
EXERCISE PLAN

Also from Harvard Medical School

Beating Diabetes, by David M. Nathan, M.D., and Linda M. Delahanty, M.S., R.D.

Living Through Breast Cancer, by Carolyn M. Kaelin, M.D., M.P.H., with Francesca Coltrera

Eat, Play, and Be Healthy, by W. Allan Walker, M.D., with Courtney Humphries

The Harvard Medical School Guide to Healthy Eating During Pregnancy, by W. Allan Walker, M.D., with Courtney Humphries

The Harvard Medical School Guide to Achieving Optimal Memory, by Aaron P. Nelson, M.D., with Susan Gilbert

The Harvard Medical School Guide to Lowering Your Cholesterol, by Mason W. Freeman, M.D., with Christine Junge

The Harvard Medical School Guide to Healing Your Sinuses, by Ralph B. Metson, M.D., with Steve Mardon

The Harvard Medical School Guide to Overcoming Thyroid Problems, by Jeffrey R. Garber, M.D., with Sandra Sardella White

Monthly Newsletters from Harvard Medical School

Harvard Health Letter
Harvard Women's Health Watch
Harvard Men's Health Watch
Harvard Heart Letter
Harvard Mental Health Letter
For more information, please visit us at health.harvard.edu.

Also by Harvey B. Simon, M.D.

The Harvard Medical School Guide to Men's Health
Conquering Heart Disease
Staying Well
The Athlete Within (with Steven R. Levisohn, M.D.)
Tennis Medic (with Steven R. Levisohn, M.D.)

THE

NO SWEAT

EXERCISE PLAN

Lose Weight, Get Healthy, and Live Longer

HARVEY B. SIMON, M.D.

McGraw·Hill

New York   Chicago   San Francisco   Lisbon   London   Madrid   Mexico City
Milan   New Delhi   San Juan   Seoul   Singapore   Sydney   Toronto

Library of Congress Cataloging-in-Publication Data

Simon, Harvey B. (Harvey Bruce), 1942-
    The no sweat exercise plan : lose weight, get healthy & live longer / Harvey B. Simon.
       p.   cm.
    Includes index.
    ISBN 0-07-144832-2
    1. Exercise.   2. Physical fitness.   3. Weight loss.   4. Health.   I. Title.

  RA781.S5647   2006
  613.7—dc22
                                                  2005027370

1 2 3 4 5 6 7 8 9 0   DOC/DOC   0 9 8 7 6 5

ISBN 0-07-144832-2

Illustrations by Matt Holt, Barb Cousins, and Scott Leighton

McGraw-Hill books are available at special quantity discounts to use as premiums and sales promotions, or for use in corporate training programs. For more information, please write to the Director of Special Sales, Professional Publishing, McGraw-Hill, Two Penn Plaza, New York, NY 10121-2298. Or contact your local bookstore.

This book is printed on acid-free paper.

To Rita

For getting me started on the path to

fitness, and for so very much more

Contents

Preface

People may exercise for any of five reasons: for work, for recreation, for competition, for a better appearance, or for health. This is a book about exercise for health.

My personal odyssey to fitness and health got off to a shaky start on July 4, 1976. That was the day my dear wife pushed me out the door to get some exercise. Without the benefit of any medical training, Rita knew that I needed to exercise, and she was right. She also insisted that my need was urgent, and she was right again. I was only thirty-four and believed I was healthy, but the warning signs were in plain view. At 205 pounds, I was substantially overweight, and my repeated attempts to diet had not countered the five or six extra pounds that I'd been packing on every year since medical school. My cholesterol and blood pressure were borderline by the standards of the 1970s but high by today's criteria. And my pedigree was even more worrisome. My father was disabled by cardiovascular disease when he was in his late thirties, my mother died of heart disease at age forty-two, and my uncles all succumbed in a similar fashion before age forty-five.

Exercise hasn't done anything for my genes, but it has done wonders for my health. That didn't seem likely on the first day, when my first jog ended rather breathlessly after just four-tenths of a mile. But Rita pushed me out again the next day and the next. Slowly but surely, remarkable things happened to my body. My stamina, strength, and speed improved dramatically. I lost five inches from my waist and found that I had to wolf down extra calories just to maintain my weight at 165, a forty-pound drop from my couch potato days. My blood pressure fell and my cholesterol improved substantially, which was doubly welcome since the first effective medications for cholesterol were still years away. And my wife was just as pleased by the changes in my personality. I felt more energetic yet more relaxed, and she tells me I became more social and outgoing.

I got hooked on exercise. From a failed attempt to jog a half mile, I morphed into a long-distance runner—quite a surprise for a clumsy guy who had never played anything more strenuous than the radio. In my medical practice, teaching, and writing, I did my best to spread the gospel of intense aerobic exercise. My motivation was sincere, and my beliefs were based on the best scientific evidence of the 1970s and '80s. But I failed to convert more than a handful of my patients, even the national infatuation with Bill Rodgers and the Boston Marathon failed to change America's sedentary ways. The aerobics revolution saved my life, but it has had scant impact on the nation's health.

After nearly thirty years on the road, my long-distance running has evolved into short-distance jogging. Considering all the miles I've logged, that's no surprise. What surprised me, though, is that moderate exercise has kept me as slim, healthy, and happy as running did—and with many fewer aches and pains.

Personal experience can be tricky and clinical anecdotes misleading, but scientific research over the past five to ten years has overturned many of the "facts" that led me to prescribe intense aerobic exercise. When I dismissed golf as the perfect way to ruin a four-mile walk, I was wrong. In fact, moderate exercise can produce enormous health benefits—if it's done right.

In retrospect, the clues were there all along. In 1978 I joined with four colleagues to establish the Harvard Cardiovascular Health Center, which uses exercise, nutrition, and stress control to rehabilitate cardiac patients. We've seen gratifying improvements in hundreds of men and women. A few of our patients actually went on to run in the Boston Marathon. That's an amazing accomplishment and a testament to the enormous power of exercise training. But the dazzle of running shouldn't blind us to the benefits of walking. In fact, for every patient who improved through running, dozens improved by walking. And in the past few years our observations have been confirmed and extended by numerous careful studies that demonstrate the tremendous health benefits of moderate exercise.

Gain without pain? It sounds too good to be true. It's not. But there is one catch. To get the full benefit of moderate exercise, you have to know how your body works and understand how to pamper it with exercise. To exercise for health, you don't have to sweat, but you do have to develop a plan that's just right for you. And that's why I wrote this book.

In Part I, I'll explain what exercise can do for your body and your health. You'll learn which exercise is best and how to evaluate your personal needs. Next, in Part II, we'll construct an individual program for you that will be effective, safe, and enjoyable. Since some readers have special needs, Part III will show how exercise can be used to treat a surprisingly broad range of illnesses. It will also provide tips for people who want to go beyond health by extending themselves with exercise for sport—and it will explain how all of us should go beyond exercise to add good nutrition and medical care for optimal health.

It's a long trip, but the rewards are huge. Let's get started.

Acknowledgments

Exercise can be a solitary pursuit or a group activity, but producing a book always requires teamwork. I am grateful to the many people who have helped with this book. At the risk of omitting some who deserve my gratitude, I would like to extend my thanks:

To my family, for their love, encouragement, and support, which sustains me in all things.

To Kathleen Sweeney Laing, who prepared this manuscript with the same patience and skill that she has brought to my other books and articles.

To Matt Holt, Barb Cousins, Scott Leighton, and Harriet Greenfield, whose illustrations bring my words to life.

To my colleagues at Harvard Health Publications, where consumer health is a passion, not a business. In particular, Dr. Anthony Komaroff's belief in the No Sweat concept made this book possible, and the steady influence and hard work of Nancy Ferrari and Raquel Schott made it a reality. Among her many contributions, Raquel designed the layouts for the No Sweat Exercise Pyramids.

To my editor Judith McCarthy and her colleagues at McGraw-Hill. Judith deserves special thanks for helping me maintain focus and preventing *The No Sweat Exercise Plan* from turning into a marathon.

ACKNOWLEDGMENTS

To the scientists at Harvard and around the world who have taught us so much about exercise and health.

And above all, I am grateful to my patients at the Harvard Cardiovascular Health Center and Massachusetts General Hospital. Working with me over the years, these many men and women have helped me translate the science of exercise into a practical program for real people.

Introduction

The Human Energy Crisis

The human body is a marvelously complex and sophisticated apparatus with an enormous range of capabilities. One of the body's attributes is the ability to exercise. More than that, the body is actually engineered to perform physical activities that seem improbable, if not impossible, to most members of the laptop generation.

In the Beginning

Think about it. Our earliest ancestors depended on physical prowess for survival. Life itself hinged on obtaining food by hunting and gathering, both strenuous activities. Finding shelter, evading predators, and coping with the whims of Mother Nature also required strength and endurance, along with quick wits.

Anthropologists tell us that at the dawn of humankind, in the late Paleolithic era, people lived in small bands that roamed over large areas to find food and shelter. Human population was sparse; scant resources, low fertility, and a hostile environment limited population to a density of just one person per square mile. Society was simple, with most members of the band performing identical tasks. The most important task was obtaining food. Typically, it was a question of feast or famine. One to two days of virtually continuous physical activity were required to obtain sustenance. These bursts of exercise were followed by several days of feasting and celebration. But even during these primitive holidays, our ancestors were amazingly active—dancing, playing, and traveling up to twenty miles on foot in a single day to visit and trade with other clans. All in all, an average day's physical activity burned up about twice as many calories as a typical American uses today.

Change came slowly in the Stone Age. Hunting and gathering remained the dominant way of life for about thirty thousand years. But about ten thousand years ago, humans learned how to cultivate crops and domesticate animals. Life became easier and more predictable. Population density increased, producing the need for specialized occupations and creating social hierarchies. Still, for most folks, the tasks of farming and herding required nearly as much physical work as hunting and gathering.

The agricultural way of life still prevails in much of the developing world today. But a scant 250 years ago, the Industrial Revolution produced incredible changes in England, and America followed suit one hundred years later. The technological revolution of the past forty years has accelerated the pace of change and has spread amazing advances to the far corners of the globe.

Life is much better (and much longer) today then ever before, but some good things have been lost. Exercise is one. As recently as 150 years ago, about 30 percent of all the energy used for agriculture and manufacturing in the United States depended on human muscle power. All that has changed. We've replaced hoes with tractors, brooms with vacuums, and stairs with elevators. Freed from physical work, people have used mental work to carry science and technology to new heights, creating a society of unprecedented affluence and convenience. But progress has its price. Mental stress is one example, environmental pollution another.

Sedentary living also has a price both in health and in dollars. Many of the chronic diseases that ravage us today result from a mismatch between human genetics and human behavior. Our genes retain most of the Stone Age imperatives, but life in the fast lane does not. Human DNA cannot provide a substitute for the exercise that has all but vanished from contemporary work stations. Human metabolism is still programmed to cope with the Stone Age threat of starvation, not the burden of overabundance. Evolution is too slow to have yet produced ways to manage today's high-calorie, high-salt, high-fat, low-fiber diets. The body has no new enzymes to fight the effects of tobacco, excess alcohol, and illicit drugs. The nervous system remembers how to respond to the threat of a saber-toothed tiger but has not figured out how to cope with a raging boss or rush-hour traffic. And as industrial pollution changes the environment, a sea of toxins presents new challenges to human genes and human health.

Molecular medicine is on the verge of making genetic engineering a clinical reality—but it can't possibly bring Stone Age genes up to space-age standards. Since science can't reshuffle your genes, the only way for you to restore nature's balance is to adopt a more natural lifestyle.

Fortunately, you can get back to basics without returning to the farm, much less the savanna. Chapter 12 will explain how good nutrition and effective stress control can help. As for exercise, the first challenge is to shake the idea that exercise means watching sports on TV, with remote controls adding insult to injury. And injury is what we get from our sedentary ways—not the muscular aches and pains that may result from excessive or improper exercise, but the heart attacks, strokes, high blood pressure, diabetes, obesity, brittle bones, and mental decline that result from the lack of exercise. Disuse of the body is abuse of the body.

You can do better. You don't have to push a plow or scrub clothes by hand to regain the benefits of physical activity. Instead, use the leisure time technology has given you to add recreational exercise to your life; you'll be rewarded with pleasure and vigor as well as health.

When you adopt an active lifestyle, you'll be healthier and happier. Unfortunately, though, you'll be in the minority, since the United States is the land of couch potatoes.

America the Sedentary

Public health experts have established Healthy People 2010, a set of national goals for the year 2010. One of the important priorities is to get 80 percent of our citizens up and running—or, at least, up and walking. Unless something very, very dramatic happens, we'll never make it.

America is a nation of spectators. Many surveys confirm what we see every day: about 29 percent of adults are entirely sedentary, and another 46 percent don't get enough physical activity. That means only a quarter of all Americans get the exercise they need.

During the past fifty years, medical science has steadily piled up evidence that exercise is vital for health, but during this time, America's exercise habits have improved only slightly. Children are more active than adults, but even in youth, only 44 percent of kids get enough exercise. Men are a bit more active than women, but both genders are shamelessly sedentary. People are more likely to exercise as they move up the educational and socioeconomic ladder, but even those on the top rung are more likely to use a lounge chair than a bike. Sloth is the rule throughout the land, but it is a bit more common in rural areas than in cities.

While we may be justified in fretting about the high prices and short supplies of fossil fuels, we tend to overlook the energy crisis that may be much more dangerous in the long term. A 2004 survey of fifteen hundred Americans found that 88 percent of adults and 84 percent of teenagers believed they were getting enough exercise to maintain good health. And 76 percent of parents felt their kids were active enough. Perhaps we are becoming the home of the ostrich as well as the sloth.

Epidemiologists tell us that three out of every four Americans need to get more exercise, but the real situation may be even worse. Most people who say they exercise report walking as their only regular physical activity, but when federal researchers evaluated more than fifteen hundred people who said they were walkers, they found that only 6 percent walked often enough, far enough, or briskly enough to meet the current standards for health. Even people who report intense activity often overstate their efforts. Scientists from the University of Florida asked people to keep a log of their physical activities for a full week while they were hooked up to ambulatory heart monitors. Some 47 percent of the subjects reported that they had engaged in moderate activity, but only 15 percent actually boosted their heart rates enough to sustain moderate activity. The gap was just as great for more intense exercise: 11 percent reported it, but only 1.5 percent achieved it. Nobody achieved a heart rate consistent with very hard activity, though 1.5 percent made that claim.

Spectator is a kind word for it. In fact, we are a nation—and, increasingly, a world—of couch potatoes.

If most of us are not physically active on the job or off, what are we doing? A 2004 study reported that the average adult spends 170 minutes a day watching TV and movies and 101 minutes a day driving, but less than 19 minutes a day exercising.

Television is the quintessential antiexercise. Among both children and adults, the risk of obesity rises steadily with increasing time spent parked in front of the tube. And that's not all. For example, a Harvard study reported that heavy-duty TV watching increases the risk of developing diabetes by nearly 250 percent, even when the effects of obesity are taken into account. And another Harvard investigation found that exercise and TV watching have opposite effects on health. Exercise raised the levels of HDL (high-density lipoprotein, or "good") cholesterol and lowered levels of leptin, a key "fat hormone." TV watching had the opposite effects, and it also was linked to elevated levels of LDL (low-density lipoprotein, or "bad") cholesterol. Add the risks of diabetes and obesity, and it's easy to see why spending long hours watching TV is a recipe for cardiovascular disease—and tuning in to medical shows like "ER" won't lessen the risk at all.

For health's sake, replace thirty minutes of daily TV with thirty minutes of exercise. As a small first step, turn off the tube without using the remote—or set up a bike or treadmill in front of the screen.

The High Costs of Sloth

Sleek home entertainment centers can be mighty expensive, but the lack of regular exercise is more costly still.

The biggest cost is health. Insufficient exercise plays an important role in four of the ten leading causes of death in the United States, including heart disease (our number one killer), cancer (number two), stroke (three), and diabetes (six). And it may also contribute to the eighth leading killer, Alzheimer's disease, though to a lesser degree. In all, scientists attribute up to 250,000 American deaths a year to a lack of regular exercise. That's more than 10 percent of all deaths—and other studies link insufficient exercise to nearly 23 percent of the chronic illnesses in the United States.

There is a dollar cost, too, and it's also substantial. A 1987 survey found that people who exercise regularly consume an average $1,019 a year in direct medical costs, while sedentary people average $1,349 a year. That difference of $330 a year might not seem like a big deal, but translated into 2000 dollars and extrapolated to the whole population, it's a very big deal. Regular exercise could save our economy more than $76 billion annually. According to *The Cost of Poor Health Habits*, a book published by the Harvard University Press in 1991, each mile that a sedentary person walks can save society twenty-four cents. And if social costs leave you cold, consider this: the book also tells us that every mile you walk will extend your life expectancy by twenty-one minutes.

Better health, a longer life, and some spare change to boot. Exercise is the best bargain in preventive medicine. Sadly, though, surveys tell us that less than a third of doctor visits include even rudimentary advice about exercise.

Humanity's energy crisis is producing a real health crisis. But we can solve the problem one step at a time. Turn to Chapter 1 to find out how much these simple steps can do for you.

Those who think they have
not time for bodily exercise
will sooner or later
have to find time for illness.

—EDWARD STANLEY, THE EARL OF DERBY, 1873

If we could give every individual the right amount of nourishment and
exercise, not too little and not too much, we would have found the
safest way to health.

—HIPPOCRATES, CA. 400 B.C.

THE
NO SWEAT
EXERCISE PLAN

PART I

Getting Ready

CHAPTER 1

Exercise, Your Body, and Your Health

Movement Brings Improvement

Exercise, even modest exercise, puts stress on nearly every part of your body. That sounds frightening, but it shouldn't scare you away from exercise. In fact, if the stress of exercise is applied properly, nearly every part of your body will respond by growing stronger and healthier. The result is true fitness. It's not measured by how fast you can run, how much you can lift, or how big your biceps are. Instead, real fitness is measured by how well your body can withstand stress of all sorts: the stress of exercise, the stress of disease, the psychosocial stresses of twenty-first-century life, and even the stress of the aging process.

Exercise can make you fit and healthy. The trick is to know how to exercise properly and then to make it part of your daily life. And the way to start is by understanding how exercise affects your body.

Exercise and Your Body

Even the most committed couch potato has sprinted to catch a bus or an elevator, and all of us can remember how it feels to exercise. Physical exertion makes your heart beat faster and harder. Your breathing also gets faster and deeper. If you're at it long enough, your skin will get flushed, warm, and damp with perspiration. Your muscles will be taut from effort, and they may ache and stiffen up for some time afterward. If you are really pushing yourself, you may notice some nausea, abdominal discomfort, or lightheadedness, and you might enjoy high spirits right after you come to a stop, only to feel tired, sleepy, or a bit grumpy later in the day.

You don't have to be an exercise physiologist to know that exercise makes your heart, lungs, and muscles work harder or that your metabolism speeds up, producing extra heat. But even though an occasional burst of exercise may enable you to catch a bus or enjoy a sporting afternoon with the kids, it won't do much for your health.

For fitness and health, sporadic exercise won't do—but regular exercise will do very nicely indeed. The body responds to the stress of habitual exercise with a remarkable series of adaptations that are collectively known as the *training effect*. Hippocrates didn't have the benefit of modern exercise physiology, but the Father of Medicine seems to have predicted the training effect some twenty-four hundred years ago when he wrote "that which is used, develops; that which is not used, wastes away."

Regular exercise will produce long-term changes in many of your body's organs and functions. But at the heart of your improvement is your heart itself.

Exercise and Your Heart

Just for a moment, suppose you've become a member of a high-powered health club. You set up an appointment with a fitness specialist and ask him or her to design a training program that will enable you to lift a seventy-pound weight the distance of one foot. No problem, says the trainer—until you add that you want to be able to repeat the feat once a minute all day long. At this point you may be offered a full refund, possibly with a kind referral to a psychologist. Even Arnold's biceps would balk, but you are far from crazy. In fact, you have a muscle that is performing an equivalent amount of work right now, and it will go on working at that level for every minute of your life. That remarkable muscle is your heart.

Although it is no bigger than your clenched fist, your heart is able to pump more than two thousand gallons of blood through sixty thousand miles of blood vessels each day. To do this, your heart beats more than one hundred thousand times each and every day of your life.

Your heart is incredibly strong, but exercise training will make it stronger and more durable. A healthy heart pumps about five quarts of blood a minute while you are resting quietly. When you dash to make that bus, your heart rate may double or even triple, and the remarkable little muscle will pump out up to twenty quarts of blood a minute. Diseased hearts can't match this performance, but exercise-trained hearts can do much more. At maximum effort, an athlete's heart can pump up to forty quarts of blood a minute, and it can sustain a high workload for much longer than the unconditioned heart can.

How does regular exercise help your heart? Like your other muscles, your heart muscle gets larger and stronger with exercise. Exercise also makes the heart muscle more efficient, so it needs less oxygen for itself. Exercise training helps human hearts resist *arrhythmias*, including the abnormal pumping rhythms that can lead to sudden death. And moderate exercise will earn all of these heartfelt improvements for you.

Exercise and Your Arteries

For poets, the heart symbolizes emotion, for soldiers, courage, and for lovers, romance. But for physiologists, the heart is simply a pump. Its job is to pump oxygen- and nutrient-rich blood to all your body's tissues; your arteries provide the delivery system that makes it possible.

Doctors used to think of arteries as passive conduits for blood, working for your body the way a garden hose works for your lawn. Wrong! In fact, arteries are complex structures with crucial regulatory functions, and they are in the front line of the battle for cardiovascular health.

Every artery has three layers in its wall. New research has focused on the inner layer, which is composed of a thin layer of *endothelial cells* that are in direct contact with the bloodstream. Endothelial cells have a crucial role in vascular health, and exercise training has an important effect on them. Among other things, endothelial cells produce *nitric oxide*, which has two crucial functions. It keeps the arterial lining smooth and slippery, preventing damaging inflammation and artery-blocking blood clots. In addition, it relaxes the smooth muscle cells of the artery wall's middle layer, preventing spasms and keeping arteries open.

Even in health, age takes a toll on endothelial cells, reducing nitric oxide production so that arteries become stickier, stiffer, and narrower. Exercise training boosts nitric oxide production, keeping arteries supple and young. And here's more good news: you don't have to start young or push yourself hard to get these benefits. For example, when scientists from the University of Colorado studied healthy but sedentary men with an average age of fifty-three, they found that a walking program produced dramatic gains in endothelial function in just three months.

More than three hundred years ago, the great English physician Thomas Sydenham observed, "A man is as old as his arteries." Exercise will help keep you and your arteries young. It will also keep your arteries healthy. The inner and middle layers of the artery wall are the battlegrounds of *atherosclerosis*, the disease responsible for heart attacks, most strokes, and many cases of kidney failure and for peripheral artery disease, which can lead to gangrene and amputations, usually in the legs and feet. As you'll soon see, exercise fights atherosclerosis, protecting you from heart attacks and strokes.

Exercise and Your Blood Pressure

Blood pressure seems mysterious to many people, but it is really very simple. Your blood pressure is the force that propels blood through your arteries, and it depends on two factors: the strength of your heart's pumping action and the resistance in your body's arteries.

Blood pressure readings seem no less obscure, but they are actually just as straightforward. Your doctor will measure two pressures with each blood pressure check. The higher number is your *systolic blood pressure*, the pressure in your arteries while your heart is actually pumping blood. But after each beat, your heart muscle relaxes and fills with blood to prime the pump for the next beat. Your *diastolic blood pressure* is the pressure in your arteries in the interval between heartbeats; it is the lower of the two readings. By convention, the systolic pressure is given first. For example, if your systolic blood pressure is 120 and your diastolic is 80, your doctor will tell you your reading is 120 over 80 and will record it in your chart as 120/80.

Doctors have been monitoring blood pressures for more than a century. It didn't take long for them to realize that hypertension is a major cause of heart attacks, strokes, and kidney failure. Even so, three very important factors about blood pressure did not emerge until very recently. First, there is no "normal" blood pressure; instead, the risk of disease is continuously related to blood pressure across the entire range. Put simply, the higher your blood pressure, the higher your risk. Second, both your systolic and diastolic blood pressures are important. Finally, new studies show that the risk of heart attacks and strokes begins to rise with systolic pressures above 115, a reading that was long considered low normal.

When you exercise, your blood pressure goes up. But it comes down afterward, and many studies show that exercise training helps keep it down. The magnitude of benefit ranges from small to large in various studies, averaging perhaps a five-point drop in blood pressure. That may not seem like much, but it's enough to reduce your risk of heart attack and stroke by 10 to 15 percent—without medication. And some studies even show that moderate exercise is better at lowering blood pressure than intense exercise. That's music to my ears: more gain with less strain!

Exercise and Your Lungs

When you exercise, your breathing gets deeper and faster. If you push yourself to the limit, you'll be panting and gasping for air. As you get into shape, you'll be able to do much more exercise with less respiratory effort—you'll "get your wind." Surprisingly, though, your lungs don't deserve any of the credit. In fact, the lung is one of the few human organs that does not improve with exercise training. The reason: your lungs have such a large excess capacity that they do not have to improve to meet the demands of exercise. In fact, you could get along perfectly well with just one lung, even getting enough oxygen to permit vigorous exercise.

Intense exercise produces breathlessness because tissues aren't getting enough oxygen and they are producing excessive amounts of carbon dioxide and acid. Regular exercise improves your wind without changing your lungs because it boosts your heart's ability to pump oxygen-rich blood and it enhances your muscles' ability to extract and use that oxygen.

Exercise and Your Muscles

Good muscular function is the most obvious requirement for exercise, and enhanced muscular ability is the most obvious benefit of regular exercise. Obvious or not, there is more to your muscles than meets the eye.

Like all living tissue, muscle cells need oxygen; they get it from a rich network of tiny blood vessels called *capillaries*. They also need energy, which is produced by thousands of tiny factories called *mitochondria*. The mitochondria are packed with enzymes that convert *glucose* (sugar) from the blood into energy; they can also generate energy from *glycogen* (a starch) stored right in the muscles themselves, and they can burn fat.

Muscles improve with regular use, but the type of exercise you perform determines the type of improvement. Exercises such as walking or biking increase your muscles' blood supply, energy stores, and mitochondrial activity. The result is better oxygen uptake and a much more efficient metabolism; you'll recognize it as improved endurance. In contrast, exercises such as weight lifting increase the size and power of individual muscle cells, increasing the bulk and strength of your muscles.

There are two caveats. Whereas your circulation and metabolism will benefit when you use any part of your body, individual muscles improve only when they are put to work. (Walking will build up your legs but not your arms.) In addition, as muscles become stronger, they get shorter and tighter. You can overcome both problems by planning a balanced program (see Chapter 8) that includes regular stretching (see Chapter 6).

Exercise and Your Bones

Your bones are much more than passive supporting structures like the girders on a high-rise. Your body's 206 bones are metabolically active living tissues. Even after you've stopped growing, your bones are constantly reconstructing themselves by resorbing old bone and forming new tissue. At any one time, about 7 percent of your body's bone is being remodeled.

During youth, bone formation outpaces bone resorption— that's how we grow. In our twenties and thirties, the two processes are balanced and bones are at their strongest, containing about two and a half pounds of calcium in the average adult. But beyond age forty or so, bone tissue is removed faster than it is restored; in particular, menopause accelerates the net loss of bone calcium in women. In about thirty-four million Americans, the result is *osteopenia* (low bone calcium), and in another ten million, the result is *osteoporosis*, a potentially debilitating disorder which is characterized by thin, brittle bones that tend to fracture quite easily.

You can help keep your bones strong by getting enough calcium and vitamin D in your diet (see Chapter 12) and by staying away from tobacco and excessive amounts of alcohol. And exercise helps by slowing the rate of bone resorption. But to strengthen your bones, you'll need special types of exercises, weight-bearing and/or resistance exercise (strength training, see Chapter 5).

Exercise and Your Metabolism

Exercise speeds up your metabolism. The harder you exercise, the more energy you use. Lying quietly in bed, a 150-pound person will burn about seventy-five calories an hour. Although the brain uses about 20 percent of the body's energy, mental work won't increase that significantly. So, alas, reading this book won't help you lose weight. In contrast, a top athlete can burn fourteen hundred calories in an hour of maximum exertion. Ordinary mortals, of course, can't work that hard, but moderate exercise will increase your metabolic rate by four to six times, vigorous exercise by more. The most obvious metabolic benefit of regular exercise is weight control. If you exercise regularly, you'll burn away body fat—but only if you use up more energy than you take in. The key to weight loss is a "C" word, but despite America's latest dietary fad, it's not *carbs* but *calories*. The math is simple but unyielding. To reduce, you must burn up more calories than you consume. In nearly every case, sustained weight control depends on eating less and exercising more. The more you exercise, the more wiggle room in your diet. Chapter 3 will help you establish your goals for your weight, and Chapter 12 will help you achieve those goals by matching your diet to your exercise.

Exercise training will also improve your blood cholesterol profile. It will lower your LDL ("bad") cholesterol and boost your HDL ("good") cholesterol. Over time, walking just a mile a day will produce helpful gains, but the more you exercise, the more your HDL will rise. That's particularly important, since the marvelous statin drugs and most other medications that lower LDL levels are not very good at raising HDL levels. Most people can expect moderate exercise to boost their HDL levels by at least 5 percent, thus reducing the risk of heart attack by more than 15 percent. Exercise will also lower levels of triglycerides, a less dangerous but still important form of blood fat. A good diet and successful weight control will augment the beneficial effects of exercise. Healthy people should aim for an LDL level below 130 mg/dL, but people with other risk factors, such as diabetes or high blood pressure, should aim to get below 100 mg/dL, and people with active coronary artery disease should set their sights on 70 mg/dL or even less. The lower the better, but sharp reductions usually require medications in addition to diet and exercise. Men should try to boost their HDL levels above 40 mg/dL, women above 45 mg/dL. The higher the better.

Exercise also has positive effects on glucose (sugar) metabolism. It makes tissues more sensitive and responsive to *insulin*, the hormone that allows glucose to move from the blood into the body's cells, where it can be burned for energy. The result is a sharply lower risk of diabetes, a major health hazard that is rising at a worrisome rate in our sedentary, increasingly obese society. Fasting blood sugar levels of 100 mg/dL or less are considered normal, levels of 126 mg/dL or more indicate diabetes, and values between the two suggest an increased risk of developing diabetes.

Exercise and Your Nervous System

Yogi Berra was on the right track when he said, "Baseball is 90 percent mental. The other half is physical."

The mind and body are inseparable parts of the human organism, and both benefit from exercise. More than two centuries before Yogi, James Thomson observed, "Health is the vital principle of bliss. And exercise of health." Regular exercise fights depression and dissipates anxiety. The rhythmic, repetitive routine of activities such as walking, jogging, and swimming functions as muscular meditation. Sharing some of the benefits of mental meditation, exercise improves the quality of sleep. Although the data are less complete, sexual function also appears to benefit. The result is a better mood, improved performance at work and at home, and increased self-esteem.

Scientists are still working to understand how exercise improves mental function. Part of the benefit may be purely psychological, the natural result of feeling more energetic and looking better. Hormones may also play a role, since exercise reduces stress hormones and boosts the production and release of *endorphins*, the body's own pain-reducing hormones that have been linked to the so-called runner's high. And a small study suggests that exercise may also help nerves carry their messages to and from the brain faster. Research is also uncovering an additional neurological benefit of regular exercise: a reduced risk of cognitive decline (*dementia*), particularly in old age (see "Exercise and Mental Function" later in this chapter).

Exercise and Your Health

More than two hundred years ago, the Scottish physician Dr. William Buchan observed, "Of all the causes which conspire to render the life of man short and miserable, none have greater influence than the want of proper exercise." History is a great teacher, but before you commit thirty minutes of each day to exercise, you deserve an update on eighteenth-century wisdom. Over the past fifty years, scientists have provided plenty of evidence that exercise is important, even crucial, for good health. Although physical activity can reduce your risk of many illnesses, its most important impact is on cardiovascular disease.

Exercise and Heart Disease

Heart disease is the leading cause of death in the United States. With the exception of 1918, it has held that dubious distinction every year since 1900. Nearly twenty-six hundred Americans die of heart disease each day—that's one death every thirty-four seconds. And that's just the tip of the iceberg, since more than seventy million American adults have some form of cardiovascular disease, including thirteen million with coronary artery disease.

TABLE 1.1 Exercise and Modifiable Cardiac Risk Factors

Risk Factors	Effect of Exercise
Smoking	None
Physical inactivity	Improved
Unfavorable cholesterol levels	Improved
Hypertension	Improved
Diabetes	Improved
Obesity	Improved
Stress	Improved
C-reactive protein	Improved
Fibrinogen	Improved
Homocysteine	None

Faced with a near epidemic of coronary artery disease, researchers have identified a series of factors that increase risk. People can't do anything about three risk factors: having relatives with heart disease, being male, and growing older all indicate vulnerability. But other cardiac risk factors can be modified to help prevent heart attacks (see Table 1.1). Physical inactivity is one of the strongest harbingers of trouble. Researchers at the Centers for Disease Control and Prevention have calculated that sedentary folks are nearly twice as likely to suffer heart attacks as physically active people. Exercise is the only remedy for inactivity, but can it also help correct other risk factors? In the case of seven of the nine remaining major factors, the answer is yes.

These physiological effects of exercise should do a great job in protecting you from heart disease, but do they actually work?

The first modern study of exercise and heart disease dates to 1953. The lead investigator was Professor J. N. Morris; his laboratory was the double-decker London bus. Dr. Morris and his colleagues evaluated thirty-one thousand male London Transport Service employees who were between the ages of thirty-five and sixty-four. They found that bus drivers who sat behind the wheel all day were 30 percent more likely to develop heart disease than the conductors, whose work kept them walking the aisles and climbing the stairs.

Although it was a landmark report, this early study was naive by today's standards. Professor Morris himself soon recognized an important limitation of the research: did inactivity lead to heart disease, or did men apply for the driver's job because they were already unwell? In a follow-up investigation on the epidemiology of uniform size, Morris reported that men who signed up to be drivers had larger waists than those who applied to be conductors, implying that they were less healthy to begin with.

Epidemiologists have now learned how to account for *confounding variables*, such as obesity, diabetes, smoking, blood pressure, and cholesterol, when they study the impact of exercise on heart disease and health. Professor Morris and his colleagues used these techniques to evaluate British civil servants, executives, and, in a second look, transport workers. In each case, exercise was linked to a 30 to 50 percent reduction in cardiac risk. And the last I heard, Jeremy Morris was active and well at age ninety.

The first major American studies of exercise and health were directed by Dr. Ralph Paffenbarger of Stanford University and the Harvard School of Public Health. In the mid-1970s, Dr. Paffenbarger reported that regular physical exercise was associated with a reduced risk of heart disease in San Francisco longshoremen. But his groundbreaking research of 1978 used quite a different study population: graduates of Harvard College. The results demonstrated clearly the cardiac benefits of exercise. The more that men exercised, the lower their risk of heart attack and death. Men who exercised enough to burn at least two thousand calories per week were 39 percent less likely to suffer heart attacks than their sedentary classmates.

Even in its initial report, the Harvard Alumni Study provided additional details about exercise and health. Until then, some doctors argued that, like Professor Morris's first group of transport workers, people exercise because they are healthy, not the other way around. But the Harvard study showed that the benefits of physical activity are not explained by genetic endowment or self-selection: men who were varsity athletes in college were no better off than their sedentary peers unless they continued to exercise in subsequent years. Much more recently, a major Finnish study of nearly sixteen thousand twins confirmed that the benefits of exercise depend on your muscles, not your DNA. The protection is kinetic, not genetic.

The Harvard research also showed that people of all ages benefit; men as young as thirty-five and as old as seventy-four were included in the analysis, and all were protected by exercise. And in a follow-up study fifteen years later, the scientists demonstrated that it's never too late to start. Previously sedentary men who didn't exercise until after age forty-five clearly benefited, enjoying a 23 percent lower risk of death than their classmates who remained inactive. Substantial benefits were linked to amounts of exercise equivalent to walking for about forty-five minutes a day at a pace of about seventeen minutes per mile.

The original 1978 report of the Harvard Alumni Study also provided important insights into the "dose" of exercise that is best for health. Death rates declined steadily as physical activity increased from five hundred to three thousand calories per week, but at very high levels, the rewards of exercise leveled off in a plateaulike fashion. Figure 1.1 shows a graph from the original publication; based on this information, doctors have concluded that about two thousand calories of exercise a week would provide optimal benefits for longevity.

Finally, although the Harvard study demonstrated that the total amount of exercise was the main determinant of benefit, it also found that vigorous exercise produced somewhat greater rewards than less intense activities. But while these insights remain meaningful and important, they are not the last word on what you need to do to be healthy. In Chapter 2, we'll return to this graph and examine new data from the past ten years to help you determine the type and amount of exercise that will work best for you.

As important as it is, the Harvard Alumni Study is limited by the fact that all of its subjects are highly educated men—almost all white and upper-income American men at that. Not to worry. In the past quarter century, more than one hundred studies have evaluated exercise and health in men and women of diverse ethnic and

FIGURE 1.1 Harvard Alumni Study

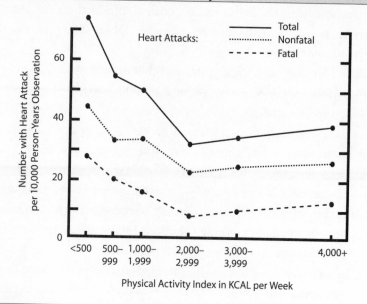

Reproduced from *American Journal of Epidemiology* vol. 108, p. 166, with permission.

socioeconomic backgrounds. Although the details vary, the conclusions of this vast array of independent studies are in broad agreement: regular exercise is associated with a sharp reduction in the risk of heart attacks and death from cardiovascular disease. Most studies peg protection in the range of 35 to 55 percent.

Exercise and Hypertension

High blood pressure is a major heart attack risk factor. It's also an important disease in its own right, causing many cases of stroke and kidney failure and contributing to mental deterioration and visual impairment in many patients. About forty-seven thousand of us will die from high blood pressure this year.

That's the bad news. The good news is that regular exercise can help prevent and treat high blood pressure. Exercise opens blood vessels, improves the arteries' ability to relax, lowers levels of stress hormones (such as adrenaline), and produces changes in hormones that govern the body's sodium (salt) metabolism. And there's more.

TABLE 1.2 Classification of Blood Pressure for People Eighteen Years or Older

Classification	Systolic BP	Diastolic BP
Normal	Below 120	Below 80
Prehypertension	120–139	80–89
Stage 1 hypertension	140–159	90–99
Stage 2 hypertension	160+	100+

If your systolic and diastolic pressures place you in different categories, use the number that puts you in the higher classification; for example, if your reading is 114/84, you have prehypertension.

The pressure-lowering effects of exercise are sustained for many hours after exercise, and people who maintain regular exercise schedules will continue to enjoy this benefit for many years. In addition, moderate exercise turns out to be at least as good as intense exertion. In some studies, in fact, less is actually more; for example, a nine-month trial of exercise in patients who had hypertension found that moderate exercise lowered average diastolic pressures by a very impressive 20 mm Hg (millimeters of mercury, the standard unit of blood pressure measurements), while intense exercise produced a drop of only 8 mm Hg. Hypertension is one of the many things that make No Sweat exercise right for you.

About sixty-five million Americans, nearly one of every three adults, have hypertension, and about fifty-nine million others have prehypertension. To find out where you stand, compare your readings with the standards in Table 1.2. And whatever your readings, remember that lower is better—and that regular exercise will help keep your pressure down.

Exercise and Stroke

Stroke is the third leading cause of death in the United States. About 700,000 Americans will have a stroke this year. Some 163,000 of those will die as a result, and countless others will suffer major long-term disabilities.

Stroke and heart disease have much in common. Hypertension is a major cause of both, and many of the other heart disease risk factors also increase the risk of stroke. Since exercise protects against heart disease and high blood pressure, it should reduce the risk of stroke—and it does.

As compared to those who are sedentary, people who are physically active are about 34 percent less likely to suffer from strokes caused by bleeding into the brain and are about 21 percent less likely to have strokes caused by arterial blockages. And in the case of heart disease and high blood pressure, moderate exercise is very effective. In a Harvard study of 72,488 nurses, for example, walking was linked to a 34 percent reduction in stroke.

Exercise and Cancer

Heart disease, hypertension, and stroke are all examples of cardiovascular disorders, and exercise protects against all three. But cancer, the nation's second leading killer, is very, very different. Can you walk away from cancer?

The answer is a qualified yes—qualified because cancer is not one disease, but many. Exercise has clear benefit against some major malignancies and possible benefit against others, but it offers no protection against many cancers.

About 1,373,000 Americans will be diagnosed with cancer this year, and some 570,000 will die from the disease. Physically active individuals have a lower overall risk of cancer than their sedentary peers. In part, this may be explained by the fact that active people tend to have healthy lifestyles; eating well, avoiding tobacco and excess alcohol, and getting regular preventive checkups all help fight cancer. But there are also biological explanations for the benefits of exercise. Most important, exercise reduces body fat, and obesity is a major contributor to many malignancies. Exercise also appears to reduce the body's production of various *growth factors*, proteins that may promote the multiplication of malignant cells. Physical activity also lowers levels of insulin, another potential growth promoter. Other hormonal effects help explain how exercise reduces the risk of breast cancer and how it may protect against certain reproductive tract malignancies. Other possibilities include potential antioxidant and immune-enhancing properties of exercise, but these remain speculative.

The evidence is best for colon cancer. More than fifty studies from around the world show that physically active people are less likely to develop colon cancer than inactive individuals. The protection is substantial, amounting to a 30 to 40 percent reduction in risk. And as in the case of heart disease, moderate exercise will confer excellent benefits.

Breast cancer is the other big target of physical activity. More than sixty studies suggest that women who exercise regularly can expect a 20 to 30 percent reduction in the chance of getting breast cancer. Considering that about 213,000 Americans will be diagnosed with breast cancer this year, that's a big benefit—and it applies about equally to pre- and postmenopausal women. And a 2005 Harvard study of 2,987 women with breast cancer linked moderate exercise, such as walking for twenty-five to forty-five minutes a day, to a substantial improvement in survival.

Exercise may help prevent breast cancer by reducing estrogen levels and/or decreasing tissue responsiveness to the female hormone. Moderate exercise will confer most of the benefit, but intensive exercise appears to add some additional protection. Like the breast, the female reproductive organs are estrogen-responsive, and several studies suggest that women who exercise may have a reduced risk of cancer of the uterus, but not the ovaries.

The prostate is also a hormone-responsive organ, but in this case, the driving force is testosterone, the major male sex hormone. Prostate cancer displays much more clinical variability than most other malignancies, and investigations of exercise and prostate cancer have produced widely varied results. Some suggest protection from modest exercise (such as walking), others indicate benefit only from very intense exercise, while still others cannot detect any link. More study is needed.

Incomplete evidence is also the watchword for lung cancer and pancreatic cancer, with several studies hinting that exercise can help. Lung cancer is common, pancreatic cancer uncommon—but since both are deadly, even a little protection would be welcome indeed. And although exercise may not prevent or treat other malignancies, cancer specialists have learned that appropriate levels of physical activity can help rehabilitate cancer patients, improving energy, self-confidence, and overall well-being.

Exercise and Diabetes

More than eighteen million Americans have diabetes. They shouldn't. Although heredity plays a role in the disease, most patients with the common form of diabetes have themselves to blame, not their parents. Guilt is not the issue, but health is. Diabetes can lead to heart attacks, strokes, blindness, kidney failure, amputations, and early death.

You can find out if you have diabetes by taking a simple blood test, the fasting blood sugar. Values of 100 mg/dL or lower are normal, levels above 126 mg/dL indicate diabetes, and scores between 100 and 126 reflect increased risk. But even if your fasting blood sugar is normal, you should take steps to keep it that way—and exercise plays a crucial role. It promotes weight loss (see "Exercise and Obesity," next), but it can even help folks who remain overweight. Working muscles burn up glucose. But the most important physiologic benefit of exercise is to increase tissue sensitivity to insulin so more sugar enters cells even though the pancreas puts out less insulin. And this important metabolic asset persists for up to twenty-four hours after a single exercise session.

Various studies show that regular exercise cuts the risk of diabetes by 16 to 50 percent. Moderate exercise, such as walking, will give you lots of protection, but this is one area in which more exercise is even better. In the University of Pennsylvania College Alumni Study, for example, the risk of diabetes was reduced by 6 percent with every five hundred calories burned up in exercise per week.

Exercise fights diabetes. How sweet it is.

Exercise and Obesity

Imagine a lineup of all the adults in your neighborhood. Look up and down the line. If you are anything like other Americans, two out of three of you are overweight or obese.

Obesity is a terrible health hazard, and, if you'll pardon the expression, it's growing fast in the United States. As our waistlines expand, our wallets empty to purchase a bewildering variety of diet books, special foods, and unregulated diet pills and potions. Everyone who shells out for a quick fix is headed for disappointment. Don't fall for the weight-loss shell game. There is no quick fix. Instead, weight loss requires a long-term commitment to diet *and* exercise.

Dr. Atkins notwithstanding, the "C" word is not *carbs* but *calories*. To lose weight, you need to burn up more calories than you take in. The math is unforgiving, the progress slow, and the lifestyle changes substantial. But it works. The National Weight Control Registry maintains a roster of people who have succeeded where so many fail. About four thousand Americans are on the list. On average, they have lost sixty-seven pounds each and have kept it off for more than five years. How did they win at the losing game? Their methods vary, but a few themes are common: adhering to low-fat, calorie-restricted menus; eating breakfast; weighing themselves regularly; and getting lots of exercise, typically by walking for an hour a day.

Chapter 3 will show you if you are one of the 30 percent of Americans who are overweight, one of the 30 percent who are obese, one of the 5 percent who are very obese, or one of the "normal" minority. You'll also learn that abdominal, or visceral, obesity (the "beer belly" or "apple shape") is particularly hazardous to your health. For now, just look in the mirror and consider three facts about exercise and body fat:

1. **Even without dieting, exercise can help.** A 2000 Canadian study, for example, found that volunteers who participated in an exercise program without changing their diets lost an average of sixteen pounds in twelve weeks. That took about an hour of daily exercise. But you can do as well or better with half as much exercise if you also cut your calories.

2. **Exercise is most effective at reducing abdominal fat.** And when you reduce abdominal obesity with exercise (and diet), you'll earn the metabolic benefits that reduce your risk of diabetes, heart disease, stroke, and other illnesses.

3. **When it comes to exercise for weight loss, more is better.** It's just a case of the math: burn more calories, lose more weight. Remember, though, that you will undo your gains if you eat more. Fortunately, exercise itself won't make that happen; if anything, physical activity is more likely to reduce your appetite than to stimulate it. Remember, too, that according to a 2001 Dutch study, people who perform steady, moderate exercise are more likely to lose weight than people who burn the same number of calories with briefer, more intense bursts of activity.

Exercise and Mental Function

At the considerable risk of sounding preachy, I've been harping on a simple but crucial theme: remember to exercise. But can exercise itself help you remember? Yes, it can.

Exercise promotes emotional and psychological well-being by fighting depression, dissipating anxiety, and improving sleep. That should help mental function—and there is more. Animal studies show that exercise can increase blood flow to the brain and enhance communication between nerve cells by promoting new connections (*synapses*) between brain cells. A study of mice even found that running increased the production and survival of new nerve cells in the aging rodents' brains.

Seven recent studies of more than forty thousand elderly Americans, Canadians, and Europeans have all linked regular physical activity with a reduced risk of cognitive decline in the "golden years." As compared with the least active people, those who got the most exercise were 15 to 50 percent less likely to suffer from mental impairment. In one study, for every mile a woman walked each day, her risk of cognitive decline dropped by 13 percent. In a study from Cleveland, regular exercise between the ages of twenty and sixty was linked to a nearly fourfold reduction in the risk of developing Alzheimer's disease in old age. And in 2005, researchers in Baltimore reported that people who carry a gene that increases risk for Alzheimer's disease enjoy the most protection from exercise.

In case you've forgotten, the moral is simple: for your mind as well as your body, remember to exercise regularly. It's another case of new research confirming old insights, in this case the eighteenth-century wisdom of Alexander Pope: "Strength of mind is exercise, not rest."

Other Health Benefits of Exercise

By now you should have plenty of motivation, but there are even more reasons to exercise for health.

- **Fractures.** Like most of the body's tissues and organs, bones improve with use. In this case, weight-bearing and resistance exercises increase bone calcium, thus preventing and treating osteoporosis (meaning "thin bones"). Do better bone density scores translate into better health? Indeed they do. Physical activity such as walking cuts the risk of hip fractures by about 40 percent in both men and women. And a study of more than thirty thousand Danes found that moderate exercise, such as walking for twenty to forty minutes a day, was as effective as more intense exercise. But although walking is good protection against hip fractures, it doesn't lower the risk of wrist fractures—that's why upper-body strength training is so important (see Chapter 5).
- **Gallstones.** Studies of women and men from the United States, the United Kingdom, and Italy have linked regular exercise with a 34 to 60 percent lower risk of painful

gallbladder attacks. Scientists are not sure how exercise accomplishes this, but several possibilities come to mind. Obesity increases the risk of gallstones, but exercise is protective in people who are overweight as well as in their thin peers. Exercise may also work by changing the composition of bile, making stone formation less likely.

Benign prostatic hyperplasia (BPH). Like it or not, most men develop enlargement of their prostate glands as they age. By age eighty, about one-fourth of all men will experience BPH severe enough to require treatment, and many others will have milder symptoms they can live with. A Harvard study of 30,634 men found that walking two to three hours a week reduced the risk of symptomatic BPH by 25 percent.

Erectile dysfunction. You may be surprised that brainy Harvard scientists renowned for advances in molecular biology and high-tech medicine also think about sexuality. But another Harvard study linked regular exercise to a 41 percent reduction in the risk of erectile dysfunction (impotence)—and all it took was about thirty minutes of walking a day. And in 2004, a randomized clinical trial reported that moderate exercise (averaging less than twenty-eight minutes a day) can help restore sexual performance in obese middle-aged men with erectile dysfunction.

Parkinson's disease. A 2005 Harvard study linked physical activity to a 30 percent reduction in the risk of Parkinson's disease in men. And men who exercised regularly early in life enjoyed a 60 percent lower risk of this debilitating neurologic illness later in life.

Ulcers. In 2000, researchers from South Carolina and Georgia reported that men who walk or run at least ten miles a week are 62 percent less likely to develop duodenal ulcers than less active men. It's a surprise, since nearly all ulcers are caused by infection with *H. pylori* (the "ulcer bug") or by nonsteroidal anti-inflammatory drugs (such as aspirin and ibuprofen). Confirmatory studies are needed.

■ **Pregnancy.** Several studies indicate that moderate exercise improves fetal growth and improves a woman's odds of having a healthy baby. Women who perform modest exercise early in pregnancy are particularly likely to benefit.

In contrast, intense exercise may harm fetal development. Pregnant women should be especially careful to avoid trauma and activity intense enough to raise body temperature.

Exercise and Aging

"Every man," wrote satirist Jonathan Swift, "desires to live long, but no man would be old." The clock ticks for all living things, and with each tick, things change. Exercise can't stop the clock, much less turn back its hands—but it can slow the tick and keep people healthy and vigorous, with the physiological capacities of much younger individuals.

To see how exercise can help keep you youthful, if not young, let's compare the ways aging and exercise affect the human body (see Table 1.3).

Exercise should help keep you young for your age. But does it actually work? The Dallas Bed Rest and Training Study, a unique experiment, found the answer by examining the effects of exercise and its polar opposite, bed rest, over a thirty-year period.

In 1966 five healthy men volunteered for a research study at the University of Texas Southwestern Medical Center. It must have sounded like the opportunity of a lifetime; all the men had to do in the name of science was to spend three weeks of their summer vacation resting in bed. But when they got out of bed at the end of the trial, it probably didn't seem like such a good assignment. The researchers tested the men before and after exercise, finding devastating changes that included faster resting heart rates, higher systolic blood pressures, a drop in the heart's maximum pumping capacity, a rise in body fat, and a fall in muscle strength. Twentieth-century American actress Helen Hayes got it right when she said, "Resting is rusting."

In just three weeks of inactivity, these twenty-year-olds developed many physiological characteristics of men twice their age. Fortunately, the scientists didn't stop there. Instead, they put the men on an eight-week exercise-training program. Exercise did

TABLE 1.3 Aging Versus Exercise

	Effect of Aging	Effect of Exercise
Heart and Circulation		
Resting heart rate	Increase	Decrease
Maximum heart rate	Decrease	Slows the decrease
Heart muscle stiffness	Increase	Decrease
Maximum pumping capacity	Decrease	Increase
Blood vessel stiffness	Increase	Decrease
Blood pressure	Increase	Decrease
Blood		
Number of red blood cells	Decrease	No change
Blood viscosity (thickness)	Increase	Decrease
Lungs		
Maximum oxygen update	Decrease	No change
Intestines		
Speed of emptying	Decrease	Increase
Bones		
Calcium content and strength	Decrease	Increase
Muscles		
Muscle mass and strength	Decrease	Increase
Metabolism		
Metabolic rate	Decrease	Increase
Body fat	Increase	Decrease
Blood sugar	Increase	Decrease
Insulin levels	Increase	Decrease
LDL ("bad") cholesterol	Increase	Decrease
HDL ("good") cholesterol	Decrease	Increase
Sex hormone levels	Decrease	Slight decrease
Nervous System		
Nerve conduction and reflexes	Slower	Faster
Quality of sleep	Decrease	Increase
Risk of depression	Increase	Decrease
Memory lapses	Increase	Decrease

more than reverse the deterioration brought on by bed rest, since some measurements were better than ever after the training.

The 1966 Dallas study was a dramatic demonstration of the harmful consequences of bed rest. It's a lesson that's been relearned in the era of space travel, and it's helped change medical practice by encouraging an early return to physical activity after illness or surgery. And by revisiting the question thirty years later, the Texas researchers have been able to also investigate the interaction between exercise and aging.

All of the original subjects agreed to be evaluated again at age fifty. All five remained healthy, and none required long-term medication. Even so, the thirty-year interval had not been kind. Over the years, the men gained an average of fifty pounds, or 30 percent of their weight at age twenty. Their average body fat doubled from 14 percent to 28 percent of body weight. In addition, their cardiac function suffered, with a rise in resting heart rate and blood pressure and a fall in maximum pumping capacity. In terms of cardiac function, though, the toll of time was not as severe as the toll of inactivity. At fifty, the men were far below their twenty-year-old best, but they were not quite as bad as when they emerged from three weeks of bed rest in 1966.

The researchers did not ask the fifty-year-old volunteers to lie in bed for three weeks, which could have been hazardous. But they did ask them to begin an exercise program, and they had the wisdom to construct a gradual six-month regimen of walking, jogging, and cycling instead of the eight-week crash course that served the twenty-year-olds so well.

Slow but steady endurance training carried the day. At the end of six months, the men each lost only a modest ten pounds of their excess weight, but their resting heart rates, blood pressures, and hearts' maximum pumping abilities were back to their baseline level at age twenty. All in all, exercise training reversed 100 percent of the thirty-year age-related decline in aerobic power. Even so, exercise did not bring the men back to their peak performance achieved after eight weeks of intense training at age twenty. The clock does tick, after all, but exercise will slow the march of time.

The Dallas study is new, but it confirms the three-hundred-year-old wisdom of poet John Gay: "Exercise thy lasting youth defends." Or, if you prefer a modern scientific summary, consider the words of Professor J. N. Morris: "Exercise is a natural defense of the body, with a protective effect on the aging heart."

To slow the aging process, as in all areas of health, exercise works best when combined with good nutrition and medical care (see Chapter 12). Just ask your doctor, or listen to the Roman poet Cicero: "Exercise and temperance will preserve something of our youthful vigor even into old age."

Exercise and Longevity

Vigor and health are wonderful, wonderful things, but longevity doesn't hurt, either. Cicero again: "No one is so old that he does not think he could live another year."

Regular exercise prolongs life. According to the calculations of Dr. Willard Manning and his colleagues, each mile you walk as part of a regular exercise program will extend your life by twenty-one minutes. The Harvard Alumni Study is even more optimistic; according to my calculations, these data tell us that you'll gain about two hours of life expectancy for each hour of regular exercise, even if you don't start until middle age.

Calculations are one thing, observational facts another. Scientists have gathered facts by evaluating elderly men in Hawaii, Seventh-Day Adventists in California, male and female residents of Framingham, Massachusetts, Harvard alumni, elderly American women, British joggers, middle-aged Englishmen, retired Dutchmen, and residents of Copenhagen—among others. Although the details vary, the bottom line is remarkably uniform: regular exercise prolongs life and reduces the burden of disease and disability in old age. In reviewing the data, Dr. J. Michael McGinnis of the Office of Disease Prevention and Health Promotion concludes that regular physical activity appears to reduce the overall mortality rate by more than a quarter and to increase the life expectancy by more than two years compared with the sedentary population's average.

CHAPTER 2

A New Look at Exercise

What's Really Best? And How Much?

hope you're now itching to get started. But before we begin turning theory into practice, you should understand that there are several types of exercise and that each fills a special need. It's also important to recognize that while we all share the same minimum daily requirement for exercise, different "doses" of physical activity may best suit different individuals.

The Types of Exercise

Exercise physiologists classify exercise based on how your muscle fibers are put to work and how your heart and circulation respond to that work. But physiology won't help you find your way through the maze of exercise programs that may point you to a gym, a track, or a yoga class. To get where you belong, consider five distinct types of exercise in more practical terms.

Strength training (also known as *resistance* exercise) builds muscle mass and power and increases bone calcium content and strength. Strength training uses free weights, resistance machines, calisthenics, or rubber tubes and metal springs to improve muscles and bones. Chapter 5 will set out a simple program for strength training.

Flexibility training is an important complement to resistance training. As muscles grow stronger, they get stiffer, tighter, and shorter. Age takes some of the spring from elastic tissue, making muscles, tendons, and ligaments stiff and tight. Stretching will help; it improves flexibility, thus reducing the risk of injury and improving performance and function during exercise and daily life (see Chapter 6).

Exercises for balance are often overlooked. Indeed, smooth and graceful young athletes have no need for activities devoted to building balance and improving coordination. But check in with them again in a few years. Age takes a toll on balance, but special exercises can help. Good balance and coordination will help you glide through exercise and sports participation and will substantially reduce your risk of falling. Chapter 7 demonstrates several ways to boost your balance.

Speed training doesn't have a chapter in this book. It's an important tool for competitive athletes who need to attain maximum acceleration and speed, but it can do more harm than good when it comes to health. Unless you are training for top-level competition, there is no reason for you to push your body to its oxygen-deprived anaerobic maximum. Still, we can learn an important lesson from the men and women who coach top athletes. They use a technique called interval training, whereby the athlete alternates periods of maximum effort (sprinting, for example) with periods of modest intensity (jogging or walking, for example). If you're like most of us, there is no need for you to sprint—but you can build your endurance by varying the intensity of your exercise, jacking it up for a time, and then throttling back to recover before repeating the cycle. You'll also benefit from varying your activities and by alternating longer or harder sessions with shorter or easier ones.

You need resistance training for your muscles and bones, flexibility training for your muscles and joints, and balance exercises for your coordination and equilibrium. But how about your heart and circulation, your metabolism, and your muscular endurance? To improve these vital functions, you need dynamic or endurance exercise. Until now, that's meant aerobic training.

The doctrine of aerobics calls for you to put your large muscle groups to work continuously in a rhythmic, repetitive fashion for prolonged periods of time. The goal is to push your heart toward its maximum without actually putting your pedal all the way to the floor. In practice, that means raising your heart rate to 70 to 85 percent of maximum and holding it there for twenty to sixty minutes. Long-distance running, swimming, and biking are prime examples of aerobic exercise.

Aerobic training is the best way to improve cardiopulmonary fitness, and it's an excellent way to promote health. On a personal note, it's what helped me overcome a heritage of cardiovascular disease and premature death some thirty years ago, and it's been a boon to thousands of people who run for their lives. Unfortunately, though, the running boom of the 1970s has done little to get the average American off the couch.

Without disputing the merits of aerobics, we should consider an alternative approach. It's not as good at improving the cardiovascular fitness that athletes prize so highly, but it's a great way to improve health. It's an approach that has often been overlooked, even denigrated. It's been so neglected, in fact, that it doesn't even have a proper name.

I was among the huge majority of physicians who dismissed this approach to exercise as too easy to be beneficial. But new data have proved me wrong, demonstrating its enormous health benefits. That's why this new approach will become the key to your program of exercise for health. Since it's so important for all of us, I'll finally give it a fitting name: *cardiometabolic exercise* (CME).

Cardiometabolic exercises are those that will improve your heart, your metabolism, your waistline, and your health. All aerobic exercises qualify; they occupy the high-intensity end of the CME spectrum. But there is another, nonaerobic part of the spectrum. To improve your health, you don't have to boost your heart rate to 65 or 75 percent of its maximum, much less 80 or 85 percent. You don't have to exercise continuously for prolonged periods. And—it's true—you don't have to sweat. But, I confess, there is a catch: to reap full benefit from CME, you have to accumulate a certain amount of physical exercise in the course of each day and week.

I know what you're thinking—this is starting to sound like every other fitness program: too hard, too complex, too time consuming. But it's not. Chapter 4 will set out a simple point system that lets you track and plan your moderate-level daily physical activities, and Chapter 8 will help you plan an easy-to-follow personal schedule to meet your unique needs.

The "Dose" of Exercise

For most people, optimal health will call for a core of cardiometabolic exercises surrounded by the right mix of exercises for strength, flexibility, and balance. It should be easy for you to see why these four types of exercise are needed, but how much exercise is best for you?

This is a crucial question, but it's been hard to answer. Doctors have debated the issue for thirty years, producing standards that have shifted over time. The culmination is a series of competing, rather different guidelines. Some of the confusion develops when a committee of experts tries to hammer out a single regimen for all of us. In fact, one size does not fit all, in part because we come in different sizes and have different needs. In Chapter 3, I'll offer a series of self-assessment tests that will allow you to construct a program tailored to your needs. First, though, let's sort through the maze of well-intentioned exercise recommendations and advice.

The benefits of exercise depend on three elements: the *intensity*, *duration*, and *frequency* of physical activity. And the amount of exercise that appears best depends on which benefit you use as your benchmark.

Exercise for Fitness

When scientists began serious modern study of exercise in the 1960s, they used cardiopulmonary fitness as the yardstick of success. First, they learned to measure fitness using the *maximum oxygen uptake test*. In order to be evaluated, you would have to pedal a bike or run on a treadmill while breathing into a mouthpiece that allowed technicians to measure the amount of oxygen you consumed during maximum exercise. At the same time, your heart would be monitored and the amount of physical work you performed would be measured. The test was designed to measure the amount of oxygen your lungs take up, your heart pumps, and your muscles use at peak effort. The result was expressed as the volume of oxygen used at maximum effort in quarts per minute and was abbreviated as VO_2 *max*. Using this benchmark, the American College of Sports Medicine issued its first exercise guidelines in 1975, calling for all healthy adults to exercise at aerobic intensity (60 to 90 percent of maximum) continuously for twenty to thirty minutes three times a week. These standards that address intensity, duration, and frequency were adopted with only a few modifications by the American Heart Association, the U.S. Department of Health, Education, and Welfare, and other authorities, and they remained in effect for more than two decades.

Exercise for Health

Although the first modern studies of exercise and health had begun to appear twenty-five years earlier, the groundbreaking 1978 report of the Harvard Alumni Study was the first to evaluate the amount of exercise that is best for *health* rather than fitness.

TABLE 2.1 How Long It Takes to Use 2,000 Calories at Various Activities

Activity	Duration
Strolling	10 hours
Housework	10 hours
Bowling	8 hours, 30 minutes
Golf	8 hours
Raking leaves	7 hours
Doubles tennis	6 hours
Brisk walking	5 hours, 30 minutes
Biking (leisurely)	5 hours, 30 minutes
Ballet	4 hours, 30 minutes
Singles tennis	4 hours, 30 minutes
Racquetball, squash	4 hours
Biking (hard)	4 hours
Jogging	4 hours
Downhill skiing	4 hours
Calisthenics, brisk aerobics	3 hours, 30 minutes
Running	3 hours
Cross-country skiing	3 hours

Turn back to Figure 1.1 to see how this was accomplished.

When doctors evaluate the effects of a medication, they always construct a *dose-response curve*; in most cases, when a compound has a valid biologic effect, higher doses produce greater effects. As you can see, Drs. Paffenbarger, Wing, and Hyde constructed a dose–response curve for exercise and heart attacks. The greater the exercise, the lower the risk. But as with most drugs, the effects of exercise reached a plateau; beyond a certain point, the effects of exercise did not produce greater benefit. In the Harvard Alumni Study, optimal risk reduction was linked to an exercise expenditure of two thousand to three thousand calories per week.

The exercise-conscious medical community (a small minority in those days, I can assure you) soon combined the results of the Harvard study with the findings of the fitness labs to promote prolonged, aerobic-intensity exercise as the best for fitness and health. With the best of intentions, I endorsed these recommendations for my patients, and I lived by them myself. In our 1987 book *The Athlete Within*, for example, Steven Levisohn and I advocated two thousand calories of exercise a week. Table 2.1 is taken from that book.

That's a lot of exercise—and it would have been 50 percent more if I had used a goal of three thousand calories a week, which would be equally plausible from the Harvard alumni data.

Even now, after all these years, I still believe that a certain amount of high-intensity exercise is best for some people. In the 1978 Harvard report, for example, participation in strenuous sports enhanced the beneficial effect of total energy output, if to a modest degree. And in subsequent Harvard studies that examined the rate of death as well as the risk of heart attacks, vigorous activities (such as those perceived as "strong to maximal") were even more beneficial than less intense forms of exercise (such as those perceived as "moderate" or "somewhat strong").

High levels of exercise are better for some people, but they can be a mixed blessing for others (just ask my legs). More important, even if high outputs of energy are optimal, they are not necessary to produce major health benefits. In fact, most people are just not willing or able to commit themselves to prolonged aerobic-intensity exercise. Fortunately, they don't have to, for there is another way to exercise for better health.

Second Opinions

Paradoxically, perhaps, the same Harvard study that helped set the gold standard for optimal exercise can also help us understand why moderate exercise is so beneficial. Let's think about health in relation to the total weekly amount of exercise, the intensity of exercise, and the duration of exercise.

The Harvard Alumni Study set the optimal total dose of exercise at two thousand (or three thousand!) calories per week. But when Dr. Roy Shephard, perhaps Canada's best-known exercise physiologist, reexamined the Harvard data, he concluded that the men of Harvard had overestimated their energy expenditures, particularly for climbing stairs and playing sports. If his interpretation is correct, the plateau for maximum gain begins at fourteen hundred calories a week, a more attainable level.

Dr. Shephard's interpretation may not be popular here at Harvard, and it may or may not be right. Leaving that controversy aside and returning to the original publication, however, we can learn that substantial benefit kicks in at seven hundred calories a week and that an exercise load of about fourteen hundred calories a week ("Harvard calories," not Dr. Shephard's reinterpreted values) is associated with a 34 percent drop in the mortality rate, a huge benefit. And in an independent review of forty-four high-quality studies of exercise and the risk of death from around the world, Harvard researchers concluded that just one thousand calories a week is linked to a 20 to 30 percent fall in the mortality rate. In all, these considerations tell us that even one to two miles of walking a day can protect your heart and prolong your life.

To demonstrate that moderate exercise is far more than second best, I've selected twenty-two studies of healthy individuals that show you how simple daily activities can provide important protection against circulatory diseases and important gains in longevity (see Table 2.2). Although a handful of studies have failed to confirm cardiac benefit, many additional studies demonstrate important gains against cancer and other major problems (see Chapter 1).

Because all but one of the studies in Table 2.2 are observational studies, they cannot *prove* a cause–and–effect relationship between a particular physical activity and an observed benefit. Still, I think it's highly likely that a causal relationship exists. Scientists have demonstrated clear health benefits of exercise in animal models. Randomized clinical trials in humans prove that regular exercise can produce a broad range of physiological changes that should improve health and reduce the risk of many diseases (see Chapter 1). Moreover, the large number of observational population studies from around the world suggest strongly that the biologic plausibility of great benefit is a clinical reality. Table 2.2 is far from an exhaustive review of these studies, but it should serve to convince you that moderate exercise is well worth the moderate commitment of time and effort that it requires.

Although we don't have the advantage of randomized clinical trials that evaluate the effects of exercise on cardiac events and mortality in healthy people, doctors have performed forty-eight such trials in patients with proven coronary artery disease. About half of the 8,940 patients were randomly assigned to receive the best medical and surgical care available, while the others got the same stan-

TABLE 2.2 Little Strain, Big Gain: Some Recent Studies of Moderate Daily Activities

Population Group	Type and Amount of Activity	Observed Benefit
10,269 Harvard alumni	Walking at least 9 miles a week	22% lower death rate
	Climbing at least 55 flights of stairs a week	33% lower death rate
836 residents of King County, Washington, aged 25–74	Gardening at least 1 hour a week	66% lower risk of sudden cardiac death
	Walking at least 1 hour a week	73% lower risk of sudden cardiac death
1,453 middle-aged Finnish men	Spending at least 2.2 hours on leisure-time activity a week	69% lower risk of heart attack
4,484 Icelandic men aged 45–80	Spending at least 43 minutes a day on leisure-time physical activity after age 40	16% lower risk of stroke
73,743 American women aged 50–79	Walking at least 2.5 hours a week	30% lower risk of cardiovascular events
44,452 American male health professionals	Walking at least 30 minutes a day	18% lower risk of coronary artery disease
39,372 American female health professionals	Walking at least 1 hour a week	51% lower risk of coronary artery disease
72,488 American female nurses	Walking at least 3 hours a week	35% lower risk of heart attack and cardiac death
		34% lower risk of stroke
30,640 Danish men and women aged 20–93	Spending 2–4 hours a week on light leisure-time activity	32% lower mortality rate
4,311 British men aged 40–59	Performing light to moderate physical activity	35–39% lower mortality rate
1,404 female residents of Framingham, Massachusetts	Performing moderate physical activity	37% lower mortality rate

continued

TABLE 2.2 Little Strain, Big Gain: Some Recent Studies of Moderate Daily Activities, *continued*

Population Group	Type and Amount of Activity	Observed Benefit
802 Dutch men aged 64–84	Walking or biking at least 1 hour a week	29% lower mortality rate
707 retired Hawaiian men aged 61–81	Walking at least 2 miles a day	50% lower mortality rate
9,518 older American women	Walking up to 10 miles a week	29% lower mortality rate
229 postmenopausal American women	Walking 1 mile a day or more (a 10-year randomized clinical trial)	82% lower risk of heart disease
7,951 pairs of Finnish twins	Exercising at least 30 minutes on at least 6 days a month	43% lower mortality rate
6,017 Japanese men aged 35–60	Walking (to work) for 21 minutes or more a workday	29% lower risk of developing hypertension
1,645 Americans aged 65 or older	Walking more than 4 hours a week	27% lower mortality rate 31% lower risk of hospitalization for heart disease
3,206 Swedish men and women aged 65 or older	Performing physical activity at least once a week	40% lower mortality rate
3,316 Finnish men and women with Type 2 diabetes	Performing moderate leisure-time physical activity	18% lower mortality rate
1,204 Swedish men and women aged 45–70	Walking or performing demanding household work	54% (men) and 84% (women) lower risk of heart attack
2,229 European men and women aged 70–90	Performing moderate physical activity	37% lower mortality rate

dard of care plus enrollment in exercise-based cardiac rehabilitation programs. The exercisers came out on top; in all, they enjoyed a 26 percent reduction in the risk of death from heart disease and a 20 percent reduction in the overall death rate. It's powerful evidence that exercise protects the heart—and what's good for ailing hearts should be at least as beneficial for healthy ones.

Is Faster Better?

Walking a couple of miles a day can help keep the doctor away, but does the speed of your stride influence your gains? The Harvard

Alumni Study reported that vigorous activity produced slightly more benefit than less intense exercise. A separate Harvard investigation of 44,452 male health professionals found that a brisk pace added to the protection of walking. But two Harvard studies of exercise in women disagree. A 1991 investigation of 72,488 nurses reported that vigorous- and moderate-intensity activities were equally beneficial. Similarly, a study of 39,372 female health professionals found that the time spent walking predicted benefit, but the pace of walking did not.

If Harvard researchers disagree with each other, it's no surprise that studies of men and women from around the world also dispute a possible bonus from high-intensity workouts. Still, there is general agreement about the main theme: the amount of exercise you do is more important for your health than the pace at which you do it. Walk or run? Either will do nicely—as long as you do it!

Is Longer Better?

The aerobics doctrine called for uninterrupted, continuous physical activity. That's why you used to see runners jogging in place at red lights (if they stopped at all) and why so many of us dismissed golf as a good walk spoiled. Not anymore!

In a 2000 study of 7,307 men with an average age of sixty-six, the Harvard Alumni Study turned to the question of duration. Each volunteer reported the frequency, intensity, and duration of his exercise, and the researchers evaluated the cardiac risk factors of each man. None of the men had coronary artery disease when they enrolled in the study. By the end of five years, though, 482 men had been diagnosed with heart disease. As in many earlier studies, the men who were most active enjoyed the lowest incidence of heart trouble, even after other risk factors were taken into account. But the frequency of exercise didn't influence protection one way or the other. The men who got their exercise in small chunks did just as well as those who exercised in a few longer workouts, as long as they ended up burning the same number of calories in the course of a week.

Is there something special about the mature men of Harvard? The Alumni Office would say yes, but when it comes to exercise, the answer is no. A study of young female college students in Wisconsin found that daily exercise was equally beneficial whether it occurred in a single thirty-minute session, two fifteen-minute sessions, or three ten-minute sessions. And in each case, the benefits were substantial. In twelve weeks the women who exercised three times a day each shed nearly ten pounds and also improved their cardiopulmonary fitness scores. In addition, scientists in the United Kingdom reported similar results, finding that three ten-minute walks a day had the same good effects on blood cholesterol levels and on stress and mental tensions as a single thirty-minute daily walk. Finally, researchers in Missouri found that three ten-minute bouts of exercise scattered through the day helped clear the fatty substances that enter the blood after eating just as well as thirty minutes of continuous exercise.

By now, it should sound familiar. For health's sake, the amount you exercise each day and each week is far more important than your choice of activities, your pace, or your timing. In the next few chapters, I'll help you make the practical choices that are best for you. For now, though, just say yes!

 ## Gain Without Strain

Armed with the new data, the American College of Sports Medicine has issued kinder, gentler exercise guidelines. In terms of intensity, they call for moderate exercise (55 percent of maximum or more for people who are in good shape, 40 percent or more for those who are not). In terms of frequency, they advise exercise on most, preferably all, days of the week. And in terms of duration, they call for thirty minutes or more each day, either continuously or in accumulated "doses" of at least eight to ten minutes each.

The U.S. surgeon general and the American Heart Association have adopted similar recommendations. It was reassuring to have uniform standards, but agreement fell by the wayside when the prestigious Institute of Medicine weighed in with a call for sixty minutes of daily exercise, and the 2005 edition of the *Dietary Guidelines for Americans* called for thirty to ninety minutes a day. Yet again, confusion appears to have replaced consensus. Fortunately, though, the contradictions are more apparent than real. In fact, a careful reading of the still-unpublished Institute of Medicine report and the *Dietary Guidelines* makes it clear that both recommend the extra exercise principally to achieve the extra benefit of weight loss. I agree. Once again, it's simply a reminder that one size does not fit all. And in the next chapter, I'll help you figure out what dose of exercise fits your size and fills your needs.

No sweat? You bet!

CHAPTER 3

Your Personal Exercise Needs

Self-Assessment Tests

A ll of us need to exercise, but each of us has unique exercise needs. For most, reducing the risk of heart disease, hypertension, diabetes, and premature death is the first priority. For many, shedding excess body fat is an important means to those ends—and that means extra calorie-burning exercise. Folks with thin bodies often have special needs, too; strengthening thin bones and building up muscles are examples. And while nearly all of us can use some help with flexibility and balance, especially as we age, exercises to improve these abilities have extra importance for some individuals. In Chapter 8, I'll help you construct the exercise plan that's best for you. In most cases, it will be simple and time efficient, and it won't require you to push yourself or even sweat. But before you start moving ahead, you need to know where you stand right now.

Let's start at the beginning, with a test to evaluate your cardiac risk. It will tell you how much emphasis you should place on cardiometabolic exercise (see Chapter 4), and it may indicate a need for additional medical evaluation before you begin to work out (see Chapter 12).

Cardiac Risk Assessment

The most widely used tool for evaluating the risk of developing heart disease is based on the Framingham Heart Study's risk-scoring system. As adapted from the third report of the National Cholesterol Education Program, the test is also available online at nhlbi.nih.gov.

You'll need some information from your doctor to take this test, but if you are getting good preventive checkups, your doctor will have the data on hand, and if you've been paying attention to your health and getting good feedback from your doctor, you'll know your numbers.

First, using the calculator for males or females (see Figures 3.1 and 3.2, respectively), locate your point scores based on your age, total and HDL cholesterol levels, systolic blood pressure, and smoking status. Next, add up the numbers to get your total score. Finally, look up your risk of suffering a heart attack.

How should you act on your risk score? All of us should do everything we can to lower our scores as much as possible. But if your ten-year risk is 20 percent or higher, you should consider yourself at high risk. That means you have a special need for cardiometabolic exercise, but it also means you should get specific clearance from your doctor before you embark on an exercise program. If your ten-year risk is between 10 and 20 percent, you are at moderate risk, and you, too, may benefit from extra exercise along with extra medical attention and precautions. And even if you are at low risk, you should know the warning signs of heart trouble, and you should know what to do if these symptoms appear (see Chapter 9).

FIGURE 3.1 Heart Attack Calulator for Men

Heart attack calculator for men

(To calculate your risk for developing heart disease in the next ten years)

I. Age

Age	Points
20–34	–9
35–39	–4
40–44	0
45–49	3
50–54	6
55–59	8
60–64	10
65–69	11
70–74	12
75–79	13
Score: _____	

II. Total cholesterol level (mg/dL) — Score: ____

Age	20–39	40–49	50–59	60–69	70–79
<160	0	0	0	0	0
160–199	4	3	2	1	0
200–239	7	5	3	1	0
240–279	9	6	4	2	1
≥280	11	8	5	3	1

III. Do you smoke? — Score: _____

Age	20–39	40–49	50–59	60–69	70–79
Nonsmoker	0	0	0	0	0
Smoker	8	5	3	1	1

IV. HDL level — Score: ____

HDL (mg/dL)	Points
≥60	–1
50–59	0
40–49	1
<40	2

V. Blood pressure (mm Hg) — Score: ____

Systolic	Untreated	Treated
<120	0	0
120–129	0	1
130–139	1	2
140–159	1	2
≥160	2	3

Total points: I. ____ + II. ____ + III. ____ + IV. ____ + V. ____ = _____

Scoring

Your ten-year heart attack risk by points

Points	≤0–4	5–6	7	8	9	10	11	12	13	14	15	16	≥17
% Risk	≤1	2	3	4	5	6	8	10	12	16	20	25	≥30

Adapted from National Institutes of Health, Detection, Evaluation, and Treatment of High Blood Cholesterol in Adults (Adult Treatment Panel III), September 2002, pages III-4–III-5. For an online version go to nhlbi.nih.gov.

FIGURE 3.2 Heart Attack Calulator for Women

Heart attack calculator for women
(To calculate your risk for developing heart disease in the next ten years)

I. Age

Age	Points
20–34	−7
35–39	−3
40–44	0
45–49	3
50–54	6
55–59	8
60–64	10
65–69	12
70–74	14
75–79	16
Score: _____	

II. Total cholesterol level (mg/dL)   Score: ____

Age	20–39	40–49	50–59	60–69	70–79
<160	0	0	0	0	0
160–199	4	3	2	1	1
200–239	8	6	4	2	1
240–279	11	8	5	3	2
≥280	13	10	7	4	2

III. Do you smoke?   Score: _____

Age	20–39	40–49	50–59	60–69	70–79
Nonsmoker	0	0	0	0	0
Smoker	9	7	4	2	1

IV. HDL level   Score: ____

HDL (mg/dL)	Points
≥60	−1
50–59	0
40–49	1
<40	2

V. Blood pressure (mm Hg)   Score:___

Systolic	Untreated	Treated
<120	0	0
120–129	1	3
130–139	2	4
140–159	3	5
≥160	4	6

Total points: I. _____ + II. _____ + III. _____ + IV. _____ + V. _____ = _____

Scoring

Your ten-year heart attack risk by points

Points	≤8–12	13–14	15	16	17	18	19	20	21	22	23	24	≥25
% Risk	≤1	2	3	4	5	6	8	11	14	17	22	27	≥30

Adapted from National Institutes of Health, Detection, Evaluation, and Treatment of High Blood Cholesterol in Adults (Adult Treatment Panel III), *September 2002, pages III-4–III-5. For an online version go to nhlbi.nih.gov.*

The Framingham risk-scoring system is the current gold standard for cardiac risk assessment in the United States. But if you read Chapter 1 carefully, you'll notice that it omits some important risk factors. The scientists who devised the system know that, too. In fact, they omitted diabetes because everyone with that disease should be considered at high risk. Similarly, patients who have had previous symptoms of coronary artery disease, stroke, or peripheral artery disease are automatically at high risk and need extra medical attention, to say nothing of extra work on their health habits.

If you are at intermediate risk, your doctor may consider additional tests to help predict your cardiovascular vulnerability, such as blood tests for *C-reactive protein* and *homocysteine*. You can also add to your assessment simply by evaluating your typical exercise level. In fact, researchers from the Centers for Disease Control and Prevention have calculated that sedentary living will increase your risk of future heart disease by a factor of 1.9 times, or nearly as much as hypertension (2.1), cholesterol (2.4), or even public health enemy number one, smoking (2.5).

Even with all these considerations, one important risk factor is missing. To fill the gap, your next step should be to assess your body fat.

 ## Body Fat Assessment

Whether your concern is health, fitness and sports performance, or aesthetics, the important issue is not how much you weigh but how much of your body's weight is fat. In medical terms, obesity is defined as an excess of body fat.

It is easy to measure body weight but difficult to measure body fat. Underwater weighing is the traditional method, but *magnetic resonance imaging* and *bioelectrical impedance testing* have replaced it for most obesity research. Unfortunately, none of these methods is suitable for clinical use, but *skin fold thickness* measurements can be used to estimate body fat. Many health clubs have skin fold calipers, and if you are tested by this method, you'll be given a goal of 16 percent or less if you are a man and 23 percent or less if you are a woman.

Sports teams like to know their draftees' body fat percentage before they offer long-term contracts. When long-term health is your goal, you'll do well to evaluate your body mass index (BMI) and your waist-to-hip ratio.

The BMI may sound like a new wrinkle, but it has actually been in use since 1869. Although it is less accurate in highly muscular men and in men over age sixty-five, the BMI has emerged as the best overall indicator of obesity and medical risk. To calculate your BMI, just follow these four steps:

1. Measure your height in inches (without shoes) and your weight in pounds (without clothing).
2. Multiply your weight by 703.
3. Divide that number by your height.
4. Divide again by your height.

Or, if you are mathematically challenged, you can simply look up your BMI in Table 3.1.

As you can see, if your BMI is above 25, you are overweight; if it's above 30, you are obese; and if it's above 35, you don't need measurements to know you're headed for trouble. But even in the normal range, thinner is better. As a wag once said, you can never be too rich or too thin.

A BMI of 22 may be ideal, but is it realistic for you? The answer, of course, depends on your starting point, but for most people, it's an extremely demanding goal. Fortunately, mortality rates don't begin to rise substantially until BMIs exceed 25 to 26, so it's fair to set your goal at 25. Even then, tailor your expectations to your body. Try to recall your weight over the years, then estimate the lowest BMI that you were able to maintain for a year above age twenty-five. Set that as your personal target, with a

TABLE 3.1 Body Mass Index

Weight (Pounds)

Height	100	110	120	130	140	150	160	170	180	190	200	210	220	230	240	250
5'0"	20	21	23	25	27	29	31	33	35	37	39	41	43	45	47	49
5'1"	19	21	23	25	26	28	30	32	34	36	38	40	42	43	45	47
5'2"	18	20	22	24	26	27	29	31	33	35	37	38	40	42	44	46
5'3"	18	19	21	23	25	27	28	30	32	34	35	37	39	41	43	44
5'4"	17	19	21	22	24	26	27	29	31	33	34	36	38	39	41	43
5'5"	17	18	20	22	23	25	27	28	30	32	33	35	37	38	40	42
5'6"	16	18	19	21	23	24	26	27	29	31	32	34	36	37	39	40
5'7"	16	17	19	20	22	23	25	27	28	30	31	33	34	36	38	39
5'8"	15	17	18	20	21	23	24	26	27	29	30	32	33	35	36	38
5'9"	15	16	18	19	21	22	24	25	27	28	30	31	32	34	35	37
5'10"	14	16	17	19	20	22	23	24	26	27	29	30	32	33	34	36
5'11"	14	15	17	18	20	21	22	24	25	26	27	28	30	32	33	35
6'0"	14	15	16	18	19	20	22	23	24	26	27	28	30	31	33	34
6'1"	13	15	16	17	18	20	21	22	24	25	26	28	29	30	32	33
6'2"	13	14	15	17	18	19	21	22	23	24	26	27	28	30	31	32
6'3"	12	14	15	16	17	19	20	21	22	24	25	26	27	29	30	31
6'4"	12	13	15	16	17	18	19	21	22	23	24	26	27	28	29	30

BMI Interpretation

Under 18.5	Underweight
18.5–24	Normal
25–29	Overweight
30 and above	Obese

BMI of 25 as a long-range vision. The farther you are from your goals, the more you need cardiometabolic exercise (Chapter 4)— and the more you need caloric restriction.

The BMI is a reasonably accurate way to estimate body fat, but it doesn't say anything about how that fat is distributed. Although excess fat is never good, some types of body fat are worse than others, and *abdominal*, or *visceral*, obesity is the most dangerous of all.

To find out if you have too much of the worst fat, calculate your waist-to-hip ratio. First, with your abdomen relaxed, measure your waist at its narrowest, which is usually at the navel. Next, measure your hips at their widest, usually at the bony prominence. Finally, divide your waist size by your hip size to learn your ratio.

$$\text{waist size (inches)} \div \text{hip size (inches)} = \text{ratio}$$

How does your ratio translate into health risk? The risk of heart attack and stroke increases progressively in women with ratios above 0.8 and in men with rates above 1.0, and the risks are substantial.

The waist-to-hip ratio is a powerful predictor of a person's risk of heart disease and stroke. But an even simpler index is the waist circumference itself—a waist size above forty inches increases a man's risk for complications, and a thirty-five-inch waist does the same for women.

Men are more prone to put on abdominal and upper-body fat, while women tend to have their excess fat around their buttocks, thighs, and lower body. If you remember metaphors better than measurements, think of them as the apple and pear shapes (see Figure 3.3). When it comes to health, though, think of abdomi-

FIGURE 3.3 The Shape of Risk

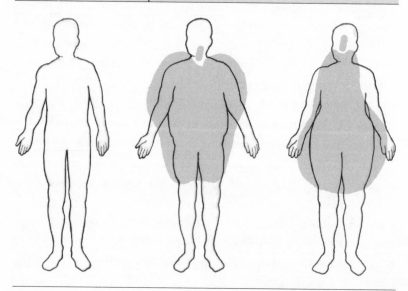

nal obesity as a poison apple, but remember that exercise has a special ability to pare down this apple.

 ## Cardiopulmonary Fitness Assessment

In Chapter 1, I discussed your risk for heart disease, hypertension, stroke, diabetes, fractures, cancer, and cognitive decline in terms of your physical activity: the more active you are, the lower your risk. Scientists have performed experiments that show the same is true for fitness: the higher your level of fitness, the lower your risk of disease and premature death. Fitness assessments require sophisticated measurements of total work capacity and/or maximum oxygen uptake. People with known or suspected heart disease should have stress tests before embarking on serious exercise, and other individuals with high risk scores may also benefit from testing. But for most of us, low-tech self-assessment tests will suffice.

Here is a minimum standard: see if you can walk up five flights of stairs at your own pace without stopping, using the railing only for balance. The test may seem too simple to be useful, but in the days before sophisticated exercise tests were widely available, thoracic surgeons used this very test to see if their patients were fit enough to undergo lung operations. In modern terms, people who pass the five-flight test have maximum oxygen uptake values of at least 20. That level will get you through surgery and daily life, but healthy people should use exercise to build up to levels two or even three times higher.

A health club would not be likely to ask you to use the stairwell for self-assessment, but it might well use a single twelve-inch step or bench to evaluate your fitness. With just a little help, you can do it yourself. Ask someone to time you and count for you so you can concentrate on the task at hand (or foot!). At the signal to begin, step up with your right foot, then bring your left foot up beside it. Follow the "up, up" with "down, down" to complete one step. Repeat at a rate of twenty-four steps per minute for

TABLE 3.2 Step Test Pulse Count

	Age	Pulse Count per 60 Seconds		
		Poor to Fair	Good to Excellent	Average to Above Average
Men	18–25	84 or lower	85–100	101 or higher
	26–35	86 or lower	87–103	104 or higher
	36–45	90 or lower	91–106	107 or higher
	46–55	93 or lower	94–112	113 or higher
	56–65	96 or lower	97–115	116 or higher
	Above 65	102 or lower	103–118	119 or higher
Women	18–25	93 or lower	94–110	111 or higher
	26–35	94 or lower	95–111	112 or higher
	36–45	96 or lower	97–119	120 or higher
	46–55	101 or lower	102–124	125 or higher
	56–65	103 or lower	104–126	127 or higher
	Above 65	105 or lower	106–130	131 or higher

three consecutive minutes. Then rest in a chair for exactly one minute before taking your pulse. Finally, use the YMCA standards to see how you stack up (see Table 3.2).

The step test can be quite demanding. If you have been diagnosed with heart disease, if you suspect you may have heart disease, or if you have major risk factors, ask your doctor about a formal stress test instead of taking the step test. And if you are out of shape or think the test may be hard for you, take a one-minute pretest to see how you fare. If you don't fare well, substitute an eight-inch step, or try the twelve-minute test, devised by the father of aerobic movement Dr. Kenneth Cooper. The idea is simple. See how far you can get by walking, jogging, or running during a twelve-minute period. For precision, it's best to do this on a track so that you can count laps and measure distance accurately. If you are out of shape, you should not push yourself too hard for your first test; instead, take a six- to eight-minute pretest to get an idea of your capacity. Wait a few days, then pace yourself appropriately during your self-test. Be sure to dress appropriately, warm up gradually, and avoid eating for at least two hours prior to your test.

Dr. Cooper's scoring system can be simplified for healthy adults to give you an approximate fitness level (see Table 3.3).

TABLE 3.3 Twelve-Minute Fitness Test

Distance Covered	Fitness Level
Less than ¾ mile	Poor to fair
¾ to 1 mile	Good
1 to 1¼ miles	Very good
More than 1¼ miles	Excellent

 ## Muscular Strength Assessment

Although cardiopulmonary fitness is most precisely evaluated in an exercise lab, you can use simple self-assessment tests to get a good idea of where you stand. The same is true for muscular strength. For a detailed analysis, sign up at a health club where a trainer will put you through your paces using resistance machines and weights. But for a reasonable estimate, take these simple tests that use your own body weight to see how strong you are.

To test your abdominal muscles, take the one-minute sit-up test.

One-Minute Sit-Up Test

Lie on the floor with your back flat, your knees bent, and your feet flat on the floor. Cross your arms across your chest, and then do as many sit-ups as you can in one minute, touching your elbows to your knees each time, then returning to the starting position. You may need to have someone hold your feet to the floor, but don't do this test if you have back trouble. Use Table 3.4 to find out your rating.

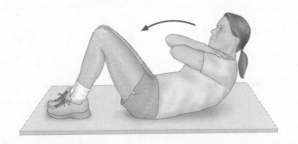

TABLE 3.4 One-Minute Sit-Up Test

| | Age | Number of Sit-Ups | | |
		Low	Moderate	High
Women	20–29	32 or fewer	33–38	39 or more
	30–39	24 or fewer	25–30	31 or more
	40–49	18 or fewer	19–25	26 or more
	50–59	14 or fewer	15–20	21 or more
	60–69	9 or fewer	10–15	16 or more
Men	20–29	36 or fewer	37–42	43 or more
	30–39	28 or fewer	29–34	35 or more
	40–49	23 or fewer	24–29	30 or more
	50–59	18 or fewer	19–24	25 or more
	60–69	13 or fewer	14–19	20 or more

To test your legs, see how many squats you can do without stopping.

Squat Test

Stand eight to twelve inches in front of a sturdy chair with your feet at slightly more than shoulder width and your arms straight out in front of you. Keep your weight back on your heels, and slowly lower yourself to a position with your buttocks just touching the seat. Pause, and then slowly stand up straight. Give yourself about six seconds for each squat. Use Table 3.5 to evaluate your score.

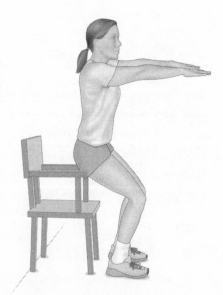

TABLE 3.5 Squat Test

| | Age | Number of Repetitions | | |
		Low	Moderate	High
Women	20–29	20 or fewer	21–23	24 or more
	30–39	17 or fewer	18–20	21 or more
	40–49	14 or fewer	15–17	18 or more
	50–59	11 or fewer	12–14	15 or more
	60–69	8 or fewer	9–11	12 or more
Men	20–29	26 or fewer	27–29	30 or more
	30–39	23 or fewer	24–26	27 or more
	40–49	20 or fewer	21–23	24 or more
	50–59	17 or fewer	18–20	21 or more
	60–69	14 or fewer	15–17	18 or more

To test your shoulders, chest, and arms, see how many push-ups you can do without stopping. Men should do full push-ups. Women should do half push-ups, supporting their weight on their knees instead of their toes.

Push-Up Test

Lie on the floor face down. Place your hands on the floor slightly in front of your shoulders. Keeping your trunk rigid, push yourself up to full arm's length until you are supporting your weight on your hands and toes, then slowly lower your chest down to the floor. For a half push-up, keep your knees on the floor. Use Table 3.6 to evaluate your score.

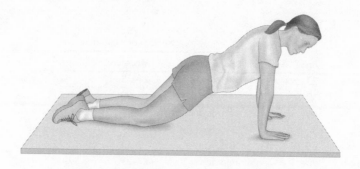

TABLE 3.6 Push-Up Test

		Number of Repetitions		
	Age	Low	Moderate	High
Women (half push-ups)	20–29	16 or fewer	17–33	34 or more
	30–39	11 or fewer	12–24	25 or more
	40–49	7 or fewer	8–19	20 or more
	50–59	5 or fewer	6–14	15 or more
	60–69	2 or fewer	3–4	5 or more
Men	20–29	34 or fewer	35–44	45 or more
	30–39	24 or fewer	25–34	35 or more
	40–49	19 or fewer	20–29	30 or more
	50–59	14 or fewer	15–24	25 or more
	60–69	9 or fewer	10–19	20 or more

 ## Flexibility Test

Because muscles tend to get tighter as they get stronger, strength and flexibility are often inversely related. In general, men are stronger, but women are more flexible. Although each of your joints has its own range of motion, you can use the simple sit-and-reach test to estimate your overall flexibility. Be sure to do some stretching exercises to warm up before you take the test.

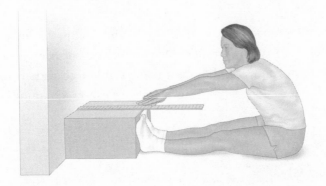

Sit-and-Reach Test

First, place a sturdy fifteen-inch-wide cardboard box against a wall. Next tape a yardstick to the box with the high-numbered end touching a wall. If you can't locate an appropriate box, put the yardstick on the floor and tape a strip of paper across the yardstick at the fifteen-inch mark. Sit on the floor facing the wall with your legs out straight. Keep your feet about twelve inches apart and your feet against the box (or on the paper strip). Lean forward steadily without jerking. With your arms out straight, one hand above the other, stretch to touch the yardstick as far from your body as possible. Repeat twice, and use your best score to see how your number compares to the YMCA standards in Table 3.7.

TABLE 3.7 Sit-and-Reach Test

| | | Reach in Inches | | |
	Age	Low	Moderate	High
Women	20–29	17.4 or fewer	17.5–20.5	20.6 or more
	30–39	16.4 or fewer	16.5–19.5	19.6 or more
	40–49	14.4 or fewer	14.5–19.0	19.1 or more
	50–59	14.4 or fewer	14.5–17.5	17.6 or more
	60–69	13.9 or fewer	14.0–17.0	17.1 or more
Men	20–29	13.4 or fewer	13.5–17.0	17.1 or more
	30–39	12.9 or fewer	13.0–16.5	16.6 or more
	40–49	12.4 or fewer	12.5–16.0	16.1 or more
	50–59	11.9 or fewer	12.0–15.5	15.6 or more
	60–69	9.9 or fewer	10.0–14.0	14.1 or more

Balance Test

If you think balance is not part of fitness and health, you may be headed for a fall as you get older. That's because balance, like the other facets of fitness, declines with age. But like the other traits you've been testing, it can be improved with exercise training (see Chapter 7).

Balance Test

Stand in your bare or stocking feet about a foot from a wall, which may come in handy if you start to topple during the test. Keep your eyes open, your chin up, your back straight, and your arms at your sides. Bend one leg up at the knee and see how long you can stand on the other leg. Use a stopwatch or have someone else time you. Try the balance test with each leg, and then use the higher score to compare yourself with the standards in Table 3.8.

 ## Web-Based Tests

At the start of this chapter, I asked you to evaluate your cardiac risk and your body fat and shape. Next, I presented tests to check for cardiopulmonary fitness, strength, flexibility, and balance. As you'll see in the next four chapters, exercise training will help you improve in each of these areas. And regular exercise can also help

TABLE 3.8 Balance Test

	Age	Time in Seconds		
		Low	Moderate	High
Women	20–29	22.0 or fewer	22.1–29.0	29.1 or more
	30–39	15.0 or fewer	15.1–22.0	22.1 or more
	40–49	7.1 or fewer	7.2–15.5	15.6 or more
	50–59	3.6 or fewer	3.7–8.7	8.8 or more
	60–69	2.4 or fewer	2.5–4.5	4.6 or more
Men	20–29	21.0 or fewer	21.1–28.0	28.1 or more
	30–39	14.0 or fewer	14.1–21.0	21.1 or more
	40–49	4.0 or fewer	4.1–14.7	14.8 or more
	50–59	3.1 or fewer	3.2–6.7	6.8 or more
	60–69	2.4 or fewer	2.5–4.0	4.1 or more

reduce your risk for diabetes, stroke, osteoporosis, colon cancer, and breast cancer. The Harvard School of Public Health has prepared tests to evaluate risk for each of these disorders. You can determine your vulnerability by logging on to yourdiseaserisk.har vard.edu. There is no charge for these tests or for the others on the website.

Test to Be Best

Most adults recoil at the thought of taking tests. But health and fitness self-assessment tests are not like the academic exams you may remember with more resentment than nostalgia. Health tests are not competitive, and your goal is not a pretty number or a high grade. Instead, you should use these tests to see how much you can improve with exercise training. Keep track of your scores, and test yourself every month or two as you get into shape. You'll find your scores improving to match your growing energy and vigor. Above all, you'll earn the only grade that really counts: good health.

PART II

Getting Going

CHAPTER 4

Cardiometabolic Exercise

The Key to Health

Chapters 4 through 7 will provide practical hands-on guidelines for the four types of exercise that are important for your health. But while all are important, cardiometabolic exercise (CME) is the most important of all. When you plan your comprehensive personal exercise program in Chapter 8, you'll see that I've asked you to devote more time to CME activities than to the other three types of exercise combined. CME is worth all that and more; in fact, some forms of exercise are more equal than others.

CME is first among equals because the *C* in CME is the best way to reduce your risk of heart disease, hypertension, and stroke. And the *M* is no slouch either, since it indicates major protection against obesity and diabetes. Add a substantially lower risk of colon cancer and breast cancer, and you'll see why CME leads to a longer and healthier life.

Virtually all physical activities that speed up your heart and stoke up your metabolism belong to the CME spectrum. Until recently, jogging was the poster child of exercise for health. Indeed, aerobic exercise remains an excellent option for health, but the CME approach extends the spectrum of benefit to less intense activities as well. That's why walking is the poster child for CME. It's not as time efficient as running, but it can give you the same long-term health benefits with a much lower risk of musculoskeletal injury and cardiac complications—to say nothing of much less strain and sweat. Ahead of his time in so many ways, Thomas Jefferson explained, "Walking is the very best exercise. Habituate yourself to walk very far."

Another advantage of the CME approach is its flexibility and adaptability. Because so many activities count as cardiometabolic exercise, you can choose the ones that best fill your schedule and suit your preferences. You'll gain convenience and enjoyment, and the variety at your disposal will keep you motivated and fresh.

CME also allows you to count small chunks of exercise toward your daily and weekly goals. You can, of course, set aside a thirty- or forty-minute block of time and remain faithful to the aerobics doctrine of continuous exercise, but you can also choose to divide your CME activities into shorter segments and accumulate those chunks toward your daily and weekly goals.

Although CME is flexible and adaptable, there is a method to the madness. The method is the CME point system.

Your CME Point System

When it comes to health, every little bit of exercise counts. But to count on getting full benefit, you need a way to evaluate a broad range of activities so you can count them up to be sure you are meeting the goals you'll set for yourself in Chapter 8. And that's where the CME point system comes in. It's a new way to account for the intensity and duration of many activities by assigning each a single number. But although it's a new system, it is based on a broad range of careful scientific studies by experienced exercise physiologists.

Because walking is the core of most CME programs, I'll analyze it separately (Table 4.1). Then we'll move on to the scores for other recreational and daily activities (Tables 4.2 and 4.3, respectively). Finally, I'll offer some tips about the most popular CME activities. And in Chapter 11, you'll be able to learn about more formal workouts that can earn plenty of CME points for people who come to enjoy exercise for its own sake as well as for health. All in all, you'll be able to pick the CME activities that are right for you. With or without sweat, the choice is yours. Either way, the result will be better health and a fuller life.

TABLE 4.1 CME Points for Walking on the Level

If you weigh this much	And you walk at this pace	You'll earn this many CME points in 30 minutes
100 pounds	2 mph (30 minutes/mile)	60
	3 mph (20 minutes/mile)	80
	4 mph (15 minutes/mile)	105
120 pounds	2 mph	70
	3 mph	95
	4 mph	130
140 pounds	2 mph	85
	3 mph	110
	4 mph	150
160 pounds	2 mph	95
	3 mph	125
	4 mph	170
180 pounds	2 mph	105
	3 mph	140
	4 mph	195
200 pounds	2 mph	120
	3 mph	155
	4 mph	210
210 pounds	2 mph	125
	3 mph	165
	4 mph	225
220 pounds	2 mph	130
	3 mph	175
	4 mph	235

TABLE 4.2 CME Points for Recreational Activities

Activity	Pace	Duration	CME Points
Aerobics	Moderate	30 minutes	200
Archery	Moderate	30 minutes	100
Badminton	Moderate	30 minutes	150
Baseball	Moderate	30 minutes	170
Basketball	Moderate	30 minutes	280
Bicycling	Leisurely	30 minutes	130
	Moderate	30 minutes	250
	Hard	30 minutes	400
Billiards	Moderate	30 minutes	65
Bowling	Moderate	30 minutes	100
Calisthenics	Moderate	30 minutes	130
Canoeing	Moderate	30 minutes	80
Climbing hills (no pack)	Moderate	30 minutes	230
Dancing	Ballet	30 minutes	150
	Ballroom	30 minutes	150
	Square	30 minutes	200
Fishing	Wading in stream	30 minutes	200
Frisbee	Moderate	30 minutes	100
Golfing	Pulling clubs	30 minutes	145
	Carrying clubs	30 minutes	165
Hockey (field or ice)	Moderate	30 minutes	270
Horseback riding	Trotting	30 minutes	215
	Walking	30 minutes	75
Horseshoe pitching	Moderate	30 minutes	100
Ice-skating	Moderate	30 minutes	180
Jogging	12 minute/mile	30 minutes	200
Kayaking	Moderate	30 minutes	160
Ping-Pong	Moderate	30 minutes	135
Playing musical instruments	Various instruments	30 minutes	60
	Drumming	30 minutes	100
Racquetball	Moderate	30 minutes	230
Roller-skating	Moderate	30 minutes	210
Rope jumping	Moderate	15 minutes	200
Rowing	Moderate	30 minutes	250
Running	10 minutes/mile	30 minutes	300
	8 minutes/mile	30 minutes	400
	6 minutes/mile	30 minutes	500
Sailing	Small boat, moderate	30 minutes	100
Skiing	Downhill or water	30 minutes	200
	Cross-country, moderate	30 minutes	315

TABLE 4.2 CME Points for Recreational Activities, *continued*

Activity	Pace	Duration	CME Points
Soccer	Moderate	30 minutes	230
Softball	Competitive	30 minutes	150
Squash	Vigorous	30 minutes	400
Swimming	Leisurely	30 minutes	200
	Moderate	30 minutes	230
	Hard	30 minutes	280
Table tennis	Moderate	30 minutes	135
Tai chi	Moderate	30 minutes	130
Tennis	Doubles	30 minutes	160
	Singles	30 minutes	200
Volleyball	Casual	30 minutes	100
	Vigorous	30 minutes	160
Woodworking	Moderate	30 minutes	75
Yoga (hatha)	Moderate	30 minutes	130

In Chapter 8, you'll learn how to set the CME point goal that's best for you. But as you look over these charts now, keep general guidelines in mind. For prevention and good health, people without special needs should aim for about 1,000 points a week, or about 150 points a day. You may need to get there gradually if your self-assessment tests show a low starting point, and you may have to aim higher if you form additional goals; serious weight loss, for example, might call for 2,000 points a week.

Table 4.1 seems to give an unfair edge to big people. The laws of physics tell us that the amount of energy required to move a body depends on the weight of that body. A 200-pound man can earn his 150 CME points by walking a mile and a half, while a 120-pound woman would have to cover nearly twice as much ground. But there is a catch. Many of the studies of exercise and health report benefit in terms of the energy expended on exercise each day or each week. These energy levels are calculated in units like kilojoules, kilocalories, and METS, which I've translated into a single simple point system. Remember, though, that other studies of exercise and health calculate benefit in terms of distance walked or time spent in physically active tasks without regard to body weight or energy levels (see Table 2.1). And in these stud-

TABLE 4.3 CME Points for Daily Activities

Activity	Pace	Duration	CME Points
Animal care	Playing, walking	30 minutes	100
Auto repair	Moderate	30 minutes	100
Carpentry	Moderate	30 minutes	100
Chopping wood	Moderate	30 minutes	200
Cleaning	Heavy	30 minutes	150
Cooking	Moderate	30 minutes	60
Digging in yard	Moderate	30 minutes	190
Dusting	Moderate	30 minutes	75
Gardening	Moderate, light lifting	30 minutes	150
Hoeing	Moderate	30 minutes	130
Household chores	Moderate	30 minutes	115
Ironing	Moderate	30 minutes	70
Laundering clothes	Moderate	30 minutes	70
Lifting or loading	Light to moderate, continuously	30 minutes	135
Mopping	Moderate	30 minutes	115
Mowing lawn	Pushing hand mower	30 minutes	200
	Pushing power mower	30 minutes	145
Painting walls	Moderate	30 minutes	180
Playing with children	Including some running	30 minutes	130
Pushing baby stroller	Moderate	30 minutes	85
Raking lawn	Moderate	30 minutes	130
Scrubbing floor	Moderate	30 minutes	185
Sexual activity	Conventional, familiar partner	15 minutes	25
Shopping for groceries	Moderate	30 minutes	115
Splitting wood	Moderate	30 minutes	160
Stair climbing	Moderate, upstairs	10 minutes	100
	Moderate, downstairs	10 minutes	30
Sweeping	Moderate	30 minutes	90
Taking out trash	Moderate	15 minutes	50
Wallpapering	Moderate	30 minutes	160
Washing car by hand	Moderate	30 minutes	100
Washing dishes	Moderate	30 minutes	60
Watering plants	Moderate	15 minutes	45
Vacuuming	Moderate	30 minutes	115

ies, men, who tend to be larger, need to log the same distances as women to get full benefit. All in all, you should stick to the walking benchmark of two miles a day, no matter what you weigh—

and if you need to shed some of the pounds that make you big, you'll do well to aim for three to four miles a day (see Chapter 8).

Pointers on Points

The CME point system may seem complicated, but its goal is to make life simple by showing you some of the many ways you can use physical activity to improve your health—and by giving you a way to keep track. Every little bit helps, but for best results, you have to accumulate enough chunks of exercise in the course of a week. And since some of the benefits of exercise wear off in the course of the day, you should do something important for your body nearly every day instead of cramming your 1,000 points into the weekend.

Make physical activity a priority. Forget something in the basement? Walk down to get it (and then walk back up!) instead of hollering for help. Meeting a friend for lunch? Walk to the restaurant—or, better yet, meet your friend for a walk. Have some shopping on your list? Park in an empty spot at the far corner of the lot instead of circling around looking for a space near the door. Walk the stairs instead of waiting for the elevator. Carry groceries yourself. Sharpen up the blades on the old hand mower instead of buying gas for its high-tech replacement. Get off the bus a few stops early so you can walk the rest of the way. Wash your car by hand. Play with your kids in the yard instead of on the computer. Take up a sport; play is good for adults, too!

Keep a log of your CME activities, and then look over your schedule to see how you can increase your point score. It may seem hard at first, but most people quickly begin to enjoy the active lifestyle. If you're like most of us, you'll be more energetic and efficient, so you'll be more than willing to trade in some sitting for walking or even some sleep for some extra CME points. Make the changes gradually, but keep at it until you bring your exercise level to where it should be.

As you can see from Tables 4.2 and 4.3, the CME point system relies principally on moderate exercise. But how can you tell if your activities are in that category? Walking is the key to CME, and when we focus on walking a little later in this chapter, I'll give you a few tips on how to gauge your intensity and distance. But there are also three standards you can apply to all forms of exercise.

Two of these methods are subjective. The *talk test* is both subjective and simple. If you are able to sing during exercise, you are working at a low intensity level. If you are breathing too hard to talk comfortably, you are at a high level. But if you can carry on a reasonable conversation (short sentences are OK!), you are at a moderate level.

Although the second method is also subjective, it is more precise. More than thirty years ago, Dr. Gunnar Borg developed the *Perceived Exertion Scale* that still bears his name. The idea is for you to rate your effort on the basis of how hard you feel you are working. That means considering your breathing and heart rate, your level of energy or fatigue, and any muscle soreness, flushing, or sweating. With a little practice, the scale is quite accurate; in fact, many cardiac rehab programs teach it to heart patients so they can

TABLE 4.4 The Borg Perceived Exertion Scale

6	No exertion at all	(like reading this book in an easy chair)
7.5	Extremely light	
8		
9	Very light	(like simple chores that don't seem to take any effort)
10		
11	Light	(noticeable effort, but not enough to increase your breathing)
12		
13	Somewhat hard	(moderate effort but not enough to produce rapid fatigue; deep breathing without breathlessness)
14		
15	Hard (heavy)	(vigorous exercise with a pounding heart and sweating)
16		
17	Very hard	(almost as hard as you can work)
18		
19	Extremely hard	(a burst of effort that you can't sustain)
20	Maximal exertion	

keep track of their own exercise intensity. Table 4.4 demonstrates the Borg scale; ratings between 12 and 14 qualify as moderate exertion.

Why does the Borg scale run from 6 to 20 instead of 1 to 10? Because it's designed to correspond roughly to the heart rate during exercise. Multiply the Borg score by 10 to get the predicted heart rate.

The final way to evaluate the intensity of exercise is to actually measure your heart rate by counting your pulse. This is why so many runners bought digital watches (or expensive monitors) at the height of the aerobics revolution. One of the beauties of moderate-intensity CME activity is that you don't have to monitor your heart rate to be sure you are getting gain without strain or risk. But if you choose to be precise, the first step is to learn how to take your pulse, using the *radial artery* in your wrist or the *carotid artery* in your neck (see Figures 4.1a and 4.1b, respectively). Practice while you are resting comfortably; because your heart rate will be slower at rest, it will be easier to take your pulse. After you've mastered the technique, begin checking your pulse during exercise. If you don't want to count for sixty or even thirty sec-

FIGURE 4.1 How to Take Your Pulse

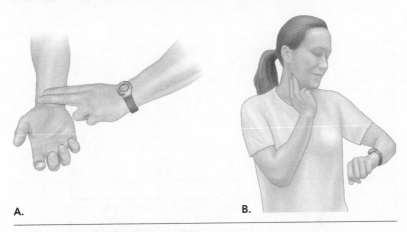

A. B.

Practice taking your pulse on your radial artery (A) or carotid artery (B).

onds, you can count the beats during ten seconds, and then multiply by 6 to find your heart rate.

The next step is to know your maximum heart rate, the pounding pace it would achieve at the top of the Borg scale. For heart patients and others at risk, that means taking an exercise stress test (see Chapter 9). But for most of us, an estimate based on our age is accurate enough. For more than thirty years, doctors determined the age-predicted maximum heart rate simply by subtracting the age in years from 220. But a recent study of 18,712 men and women of all ages has produced a more precise formula:

$$\text{maximum heart rate} = 208 - (0.7 \times \text{age in years})$$

Instead of wasting valuable exercise time doing the math, you can look up your predicted maximum heart rate in Table 4.5. In the

TABLE 4.5 Your Target Heart Rate

Age	Predicted Maximum Heart Rate	Target Heart Rate		
		55% Maximum	70% Maximum	85% Maximum
20	194	107	136	165
25	191	105	134	162
30	187	103	131	159
35	184	101	129	156
40	180	99	126	153
45	177	97	124	150
50	173	95	121	147
55	170	94	119	145
60	166	91	116	141
65	163	90	114	139
70	159	87	112	135
75	155	85	109	132
80	152	84	106	129

Moderate intensity   Aerobic intensity

Cardiometabolic benefit

same chart you'll find the target rates for aerobic exercise, which is generally pegged at 70 to 85 percent of maximum. And you'll also find the No Sweat range for moderate exercise; heart rates of 55 to 70 percent of maximum will produce plenty of gain without strain.

If you stick with moderate CME activities, you'll never really need to check your pulse. Still, Table 4.5 is a useful demonstration of the broad range of exercise intensities that will bolster your health.

 ## Get Started

Cardiometabolic exercise is about not math but health. Now it's time to turn from this river of numbers to the ocean of health.

People who played sports in school but slid into sloth after graduation may be tempted to bite off more than they can chew. If you try to get back into shape by joining the neighborhood teens in a full-court basketball game, you'll be courting injury (and embarrassment), not health. On the other hand, people who have never been active may find any exercise intimidating. So the best approach for all of you is to check your self-assessment tests from Chapter 3, pick an activity that feels right, and start modestly. If you keep at it, though, you'll build up surprisingly quickly.

Guidance is always welcome. Fortunately, you don't need to invest in a health club or personal trainer to get started, though both can help you move to the next level (see Chapter 11). Try to hook up with a neighbor or relative who has learned to exercise for health; most are true believers who will be glad to share their knowledge and experience. You can also learn a lot from members of the younger generation who are athletically inclined.

Exercise classes are available at many community centers, schools, and Ys. They can help keep you motivated and are particularly valuable for strength and flexibility training (see Chapters 5 and 6). Programs ranging from aerobic dance to aquadynamics can also help with cardiometabolic exercise, but group programs are not necessary. In fact, studies performed in Philadelphia and Dallas have demonstrated that self-directed lifestyle activities can achieve weight loss, risk factor reductions, and improved cardiopulmonary fitness every bit as well as supervised structured exercise programs.

One of the virtues of the CME program is that you can use a wide range of activities to preserve and improve your health. Look over the menu, and then choose the options that suit you best. In planning your exercise, consider your body type and personal goals, your schedule, and the facilities and supports at your disposal. Best of all, investigate a number of activities so you can get your daily points in at home or away, during crunch time and vacations, and in weather that's harsh or hospitable.

For the rest of the chapter, I'll discuss some popular CME options, starting with the key to most programs: walking. You'll find information on more intense CME activities in Chapter 11 and tips on how to make it all fit in Chapter 8.

Walk to Health

Walking has it all. Simple and natural, it doesn't require any instruction or skill. It can be a very modest form of exercise for people who are out of shape or intense enough to be an Olympic sport. You can walk alone for solitude or with companions for friendship. You can walk indoors on a treadmill or outside in the city or country, at home or away. You can get all the benefits of cardiometabolic exercise with a very low risk of injury. And to boot, walking is inexpensive. All things considered, Charles Dickens got it right: "Walk to be happy, walk to be healthy."

Walk for Transportation

Make walking part of your daily life. If it's not too far, walk to work and to the store. Try walking to the train instead of driving, and get off the bus or subway a few stops before your destination. Instead of competing for the closest parking space or paying for the nearest lot, park farther away and walk to your destination. Go for a walk at lunchtime instead of spending all your time in the cafeteria.

You don't need any special equipment to walk in the course of your daily life. Supportive street shoes will suffice, but if you wear fashion shoes, consider changing into walking shoes for your commute or lunchtime stroll. And since you don't need to push yourself enough to sweat, you don't need special clothing; just stay warm in the winter, cool in the summer, and dry in the rain. But when the weather is really harsh or the street slippery, put safety first and walk down long hallways, in a mall, or on the stairs (see "Climb to Health").

Does walking for transportation pay off? And how. A recent study of twelve thousand adults found that people who live in cities have a lower risk of being overweight and obese than people who live in the suburbs. In Atlanta, for example, 45 percent of suburban men were overweight and 23 percent were obese; among urbanites, however, only 37 percent were overweight and 13 percent obese. The explanation: driving versus walking.

As a rule of thumb, urban walkers can count twelve average city blocks as one mile. Another way to keep track of your distance is to buckle a pedometer to your belt. Some pedometers just keep track of your steps, while others have bells and whistles, such as timers, clocks, alarms, and bells—or, at least, chimes that ring out little tunes. You can get a decent pedometer for under $40, but even the best models can sometimes mistake a jiggle for a step. Still, a pedometer can help you keep track and can motivate you to take extra steps whenever you can. For people with average stride lengths, count two thousand steps as about a mile of walking. And if you are counting steps, you can use another rule of thumb to estimate your intensity: eighty steps a minute indicates a leisurely pace; one hundred steps a minute, a moderate to brisk pace; and 120 steps a minute, a fast pace. Even without counting, you'll do well simply by reminding yourself to walk briskly. It's the only direction that researchers gave to a group of eighty-four overweight, sedentary volunteers, yet even without athletic experience, all of them achieved heart rates in the moderate (58 to 70 percent of maximum) range.

In this high-tech era, technologically inspired workouts are the rage. For example, when George W. Bush took over the White House, he installed a treadmill on Air Force One. Like his father, Mr. Bush is athletic, fit, and dedicated to exercise and sports. Politics notwithstanding, both Presidents Bush set fine examples of exercise for maximum fitness. But, putting partisan politics aside, President Harry S Truman's daily "constitutionals" set a fine example of walking for health and pleasure (to say nothing of votes) in the course of daily life.

Walking for transportation is a good way to start any exercise program, and it will always remain a valuable way to add CME points to every plan. It's also smart to set aside dedicated time to walk for exercise, health, and pleasure.

Walk for Walking

Whether you walk in a business suit or sweat suit, on city streets or country roads, it's still the same left, right, left for health. In fact, it's not a question of either-or, since every walk you take is a step toward good health. Still, I encourage you to set aside some time to walk for health and pleasure.

Walking for walking's sake shows you are giving exercise the priority it deserves. It will get you away from the demanding routines of daily life, a nice plus for mental health. And by changing into walking shoes and athletic togs, you'll be able to work up to a pace that's difficult to achieve on the way to work.

Good shoes are important. Most major athletic brands offer shoes especially designed for walking. Fit and comfort are more important than style; your shoes should feel supportive but not snug or constricting. Look for a padded tongue and heel counter. The uppers should be light, breathable, and flexible; the insole, moisture resistant; and the sole, shock absorbent. The heel wedge should be raised so the sole at the back of the shoe is two times thicker than at the front. Finally, the toe box should be roomy, even when you're wearing athletic socks.

Your goals are worth a little thought, but your clothing is strictly a matter of common sense and personal preference. A T-shirt and shorts are fine in warm weather. An ordinary sweat suit will do nicely when it's cool, but a nylon athletic suit may be more comfortable. Add layers as the temperature drops; gloves and a hat are particularly important. If you really get into it, a water-repellant suit of Gore-Tex or a similar synthetic fabric will keep you warm without getting soggy with sweat.

For safety's sake, pick brightly colored outer garments, and always wear a reflector on country roads if it's dark. Walk facing cars if you don't have a sidewalk underfoot, and avoid high-speed and congested traffic. Beware of dogs and, for that matter, people; in particular, women who plan to walk in unfamiliar locales or remote areas should check with authorities first and should try to walk with a companion.

Stretch to warm up before you walk and again to cool down afterward (see Chapter 6). Start out at a slow pace, and slow down toward the end of your walk as well. Begin with routes that are well within your range, and then extend your distances as you improve. The same is true of your pace; begin modestly, and then pick up your speed as you get into shape. Intersperse a brisk clip with a less strenuous stride, and then gradually extend these speedier intervals. Add a few hills for variety and for additional intensity.

One of the nice things about walking is that you don't need special skill, much less lessons. Still, a few tips may help you get the hang of it. Try to keep your posture erect with your chin up, your eyes forward, and your shoulders square. Keep your back straight, belly flat, and buttocks tucked in. Keep your arms close to your torso, bent at the elbow. Take a natural stride, but try to lengthen your stride as you improve. Land on your heels, and then roll forward to push off with your toes. Swing your arms with each stride, and keep up a steady rhythmic cadence.

To stay motivated, walk with a friend or listen to a radio or tape. For some people, the best motivation is a dog. Studies show that owning pets is good for health, and walking the dog is a major reason for this benefit.

To avoid problems, back off if you are ill or injured, always listen to your body, stay well hydrated, and avoid hazardous conditions (see Chapter 9). Consider walking in a mall if it's too hot, cold, wet, or slippery outdoors. You can also consider using a treadmill at home or at a health club (see Chapter 11).

Climb to Health

Stair-climbing is the best-kept secret in exercise for health. It is a great way to add CME points during the course of daily life, and it will help improve your leg strength and balance (see Chapters 5 and 7, respectively), as well as your heart and waistline.

By way of example, let me tell you the story of Lewis Ripps. Lew is a trim seventy-two-year-old businessman who runs six and a half miles a day along the hilly Berkshire roads when he is at his Massachusetts vacation home. But he's in Massachusetts only for most summer and autumn weekends and for occasional weekends during the rest of the year. At home in New Jersey, Lew doesn't run—nor does he swim, bike, use exercise machines, or walk for health.

Mr. Ripps seems to be a weekend warrior who is breaking all the rules. At any age, sporadic intense exercise is a bad idea, and at age seventy-two, it's an invitation for disaster (see Chapter 9). But Lew is quite safe because he stays active the year round—not through any formal exercise program, but by walking stairs. And he does quite a lot of that; in fact, he averages eighteen long, steep flights a day at the New Jersey manufacturing plant he manages.

Coaches, cardiologists, and housewives have long been in on the secrets of stairs. Many football coaches "ask" their players to charge up flight after flight of stadium steps to get in shape, and other competitive athletes put gymnasium stairwells to similar use.

In the days before stress testing held sway, doctors would often walk up stairs with patients to check their cardiopulmonary function. Even today, cardiologists tell patients they are fit enough to have sex if they can walk up two or three flights comfortably, and surgeons may clear patients for lung operations if they can manage five or six flights. As for housewives, taking care of a two- or three-story home is one reason American women outlive their husbands by an average of 5.4 years.

What's so special about stairs? Researchers in Canada answered the question by monitoring seventeen healthy male volunteers with an average age of sixty-four while they walked, lifted weights, or climbed stairs. Stair-climbing was the most demanding. It was twice as taxing as brisk walking on the level and 50 percent harder than walking up a steep incline or lifting weights. And peak exertion was attained much faster by climbing stairs than by walking, which is why nearly everyone huffs and puffs going up stairs, at least until their second wind kicks in after a few flights.

Because stairs are so taxing, only the very young at heart should attempt to charge up long flights. But at a slow, steady pace, stairs can be a health plus for the rest of us. Begin modestly with a flight or two, and then escalate as you improve. Take the stairs whenever you can; if you have a long way to go, walk partway, and then switch to an elevator. Use the railing for balance and security (especially going down), and don't try the stairs after a heavy meal or if you feel unwell.

Even at a slow pace, you'll earn CME points two to three times faster climbing stairs than walking briskly on the level. The Harvard Alumni Study found that men who average at least eight flights a day enjoy a 33 percent lower mortality rate than men who are sedentary—and that's even better than the 22 percent lower death rate men earned by walking 1.3 miles a day. That may be a bit optimistic, but even if you don't count on just eight flights a day to keep you healthy, you should add stairs to your CME menu at every opportunity.

Want to stay well? Step right up!

Swing to Health

Unlike walking and stair-climbing, golf is a sport that requires skill, training, and practice. But I'm including it in this chapter on cardiometabolic exercise because it gives me a chance to correct myself. On countless occasions in the 1970s, '80s, and even early '90s, I proclaimed that golf is a perfect way to spoil a four-mile walk. That's because the aerobics doctrine insisted that the health benefits of exercise depend on continuous, brisk activity. Golf is anything but aerobic. Still, it can be excellent for your health—if you walk the course.

Finland is hardly the golf capital of the world, but scientists there conducted a study that shows the sport really can promote fitness and health. The subjects were 110 healthy but sedentary men between the ages of forty-eight and sixty-four. During the trial, half the men played eighteen holes of golf two to three times a week, always walking the course. The other men didn't play golf, but they did continue their normal routines, which sometimes included gardening and household chores. All the men went through a series of tests before and after the twenty-week experiment. In just that short period, the golfers had pulled ahead, losing weight, reducing their girth and abdominal fat, improving their aerobic exercise capacity as measured by treadmill tests, increasing muscular strength as measured by back extension, and boosting their HDL ("good") cholesterol levels. The golfers also showed a tendency toward reduced blood pressure, but these changes, unlike the others, did not meet tough statistical standards for validity. More good news: the men who shouted fore were rarely sore, since golf injuries were minimal. And if the Finnish experiment doesn't convince you that cartless golf can be good for health, consider another study—one that shows golf can develop balance as well as tai chi can (see Chapter 7).

Golf may be good for healthy men, but is it also safe for men with ailing hearts? Another European study, this time from Germany, is reassuring. Doctors carefully monitored twenty men with heart disease during and after a round of competitive golf. The physical stress of pulling their clubs over eighteen hilly holes and the mental stress of competition boosted the players' heart rates to an average of 105 beats per minute, which is almost at the aerobic target of 109 for men at age sixty-five. Playing golf was also strenuous enough to boost the players' blood pressures and adrenaline levels. Even so, competitive golf was easy on the heart: all the men wore heart monitors, and none developed abnormal heart rhythms or cardiac symptoms during the study.

Golf is good for your health and safe for your heart, but if you're not used to walking, you shouldn't switch from riding in a cart to walking eighteen holes all at once. Instead, get in shape for golf before you use golf to stay in shape. Start walking for health, and then walk for nine holes once or twice a week. If you build up slowly, you'll be able to make the transition from riding to walking without a bogie, at least where your health is concerned.

Golf is not for everyone, but if you are in the swing, consider these tips to help your game as well as your health:

- **Get in shape for golf before you count on golf to keep you fit.** Walk to build up your cardiovascular endurance, and do exercises for flexibility and strength. Your health will improve, and so will your game.
- **Stretch.** As muscles are used, they get stronger, but also tighter and stiffer. Age, too, takes a toll on flexibility. Stretching will help reduce your risk of injury and help you develop a smoother stroke. You'll reap similar advantages off the links (see Chapter 6).
- **Build strong muscles and bone.** We all lose muscle mass and bone calcium as we age. Strength training will reverse the trend (see Chapter 5), especially if it's accompanied by the right amount of protein, calcium, and vitamin D in your diet (see Chapter 12).
- **Warm up.** Cold muscles and ligaments are vulnerable to injury; warming up really will help—and it will also improve your swing. An Australian study of 1,040 golfers

reported that nearly half didn't warm up at all, and most of the others did little more than take a few practice swings. Walking and calisthenics will bring your circulation up to speed, and stretching will loosen up your muscles and joints. Spend ten to fifteen minutes warming up even before you start your practice swings. Join the 3 percent of golfers who warm up properly—it will suit you to a tee.

- **Take lessons.** Good technique is your best defense against both injuries and high scores.
- **Use good equipment.** Golfers pay lots of attention to their clubs, but many overlook the importance of their shoes, socks, gloves, and clothing.
- **Spot problems early and treat them aggressively.** You can play through minor aches and pains, but remember to ice down aching tissues as soon as you get to the clubhouse. Use the PRICE (protection, rest, ice, compression, elevation) approach to treat more serious problems, and get help from a trainer, physical therapist, or doctor if you don't improve promptly (see Chapter 9).
- **Don't neglect the little things.** Stay well hydrated, but don't eat a full meal before a game. Protect yourself from the sun (wear a wide-brimmed hat, long sleeves if it's not too hot, sunscreen with an SPF of 15 or higher, and sunglasses) and from insects (use a repellant containing DEET).
- **Enjoy the nineteenth hole, but don't undermine your gains with ill-advised food or drink.** Remember that a good diet and moderate exercise always make a winning twosome.

Ride to Health

Biking shares many of the advantages of walking. It can be leisurely or intense, solitary or social, purely recreational or functional enough for commuting to work and doing errands around town. Walkers can escape the elements on a treadmill, bikers on a stationary bike. Both biking and walking are splendid CME activities. But for all these similarities, biking and walking also have important differences.

The most obvious difference is biking's dependence on equipment. Long gone are the days when your trusty red Schwinn was your only option. Today's riders have the luxury—and dilemma—of choosing between road bikes, touring bikes, hybrids, recumbents, and racers. And that's not all: frames may be steel or aluminum, tires fat or thin, seats wide or narrow, handlebars upright or dropped down, pedals equipped with toe clips or clipless. You can get a bike for a few hundred bucks at Wal-Mart, or you can spend $1,500 for a Trek Fuel 90 like George W. Bush or $8,000 for a custom Ottrott like John F. Kerry.

Another difference is that biking requires some instruction and skill. Most Americans learn how to ride in youth, and most adults retain the ability. But if riding is a distant memory, give yourself some time to get back in the groove.

The most important difference between walking and biking is safety. Biking is the most popular sport in America, and it's also one of the most hazardous. Most injuries occur because riders are careless about road conditions, automobiles, or rules of the road, but others are caused by dangerous drivers, careless pedestrians, or equipment failure. Always wear a top-quality helmet when you ride. Obey traffic laws, and ride attentively and defensively. Avoid hazardous conditions and excess speed. Use reflectors and lights when it's dark, and beware of dogs, road hazards, and parked cars, which can knock you down if a passenger suddenly opens a door.

Biking gives you a lot to worry about, but it also gives you a lot of benefit. It's a wonderful form of exercise for people of all ages and fitness levels. It's a great family activity. It's a good way to get around town or get away.

If biking is your speed, spend some time selecting the bike that's best for you. Bike shops are generally more expensive than department stores, but shop employees will help you pick the right model and be sure you get the right size. Start slowly, improve gradually, and then pedal your way to health. And if all this seems too complex, consider riding that old warhorse of fitness, the stationary bike, either at home or at a gym (see Chapter 11).

Splash to Health

Life on earth evolved from the water. It is perhaps appropriate that humans should return to the water for exercise and health.

In many ways, swimming is the ideal form of exercise. Like the other CME activities, it's good for your circulation and metabolism. Unlike walking and biking, however, swimming uses the back, upper body, and arms, so it builds balanced muscular strength and endurance. Swimming also has the unique advantage of increasing the flexibility of your muscles, ligaments, and joints. Above all, swimming is easy on your body. Because water is buoyant, it supports your body's weight, greatly reducing the risk of injury.

For all its assets, swimming has four drawbacks.

First, it requires the ability to swim. Anyone can learn, and it's never too late to take lessons. But it takes time and effort to learn to swim well, and some of the people who could benefit most from swimming find it difficult to acquire this skill. Fortunately, there are excellent aquatic alternatives. Aquadynamics are water exercises that can be performed by nonswimmers. Many community pools and Ys offer instruction and group classes. Another way to get a great workout in water is to wear a buoyant vest or belt, which allows nonswimmers to stay afloat so they can run in water, getting all the benefits of running without any of the trauma.

The second drawback to swimming is the risk of drowning. It's a small risk, but it must be taken seriously.

The third drawback is the hardest to overcome: to swim, you need water. Before you can work out in the water, you have to get to the water. The logistics can be difficult, but this problem, too, can be solved. Look for a lake or community pool in summer and an indoor high school, Y, or health club pool for use during the cool months.

The final drawback to swimming is that it lacks some of the benefits of weight-bearing exercises. It is not effective for building bone calcium and skeletal strength, and it's less efficient for weight loss. Still, it's excellent for improving cholesterol and blood sugar metabolism as well as for cardiovascular conditioning and muscle endurance—with a very low risk of injury.

Lap swimming is a solitary activity. At first, it may seem boring, but the peacefulness can be relaxing, and the rhythmic exercise, invigorating. Consider getting in the swim of things for fitness, health, and pleasure.

 ## Waltz to Health

Aerobic dance is now widely accepted as a moderate-to-intense CME activity (see Chapter 11). But the aerobic doctrine that gave rise to aerobic dance also heaped scorn on ballroom dancing for health. Wrong again! You won't break into a sweat (unless you mash a toe!), but you'll get nice CME benefits, to say nothing of companionship and pleasure. Line dancing and square dancing are more intense. Swing your partner, improve your health.

 ## Glide to Health

Ice-skating, roller-skating, skateboarding, and roller-blading are all valuable forms of exercise. They can earn plenty of CME points while conditioning your leg muscles, getting you outdoors, and providing fun and companionship. They do require equipment that can be somewhat costly, and they demand moderate levels of skill and coordination. Falls and accidents, alas, are among the other drawbacks of skating. Still, skating is a familiar activity that can slide nicely into the less familiar role of exercise for health's sake.

Just Do It for Health

By now you get the idea. Gardening, tai chi, and table tennis all count. You don't have to be a jock to exercise for health. On the contrary, the CME system points out that nearly any form of physical activity will help prevent major illnesses and premature death. More than that, exercise will help you feel good and look good.

The choice is yours. If you like sports, you'll be glad to know that play has serious benefits. If you have strenuous chores to do, the knowledge that you're working for your health may take some of the curse off scrubbing the floor. If you like bowling, you can strike back at the exercise gurus who spared your sport no scorn. If you like music, you can pick up the beat of Scott Simons, my barber, who spends three hours a day at "aerobic drumming" to preserve his health as well as to fine-tune his performances.

Any choice is fine—as long as you say yes. Use the self-assessment tests in Chapter 3 to determine your starting point and needs, use common sense to figure out what activities best fit your abilities and schedule, and then use Tables 4.1 through 4.3 to learn how to accumulate the CME points you need. Remember, too, that strength training, stretching, and balance training have important health benefits. We'll look at these in the next three chapters and then put it all together in a program that really is simple and efficient. And if you get to like exercise for its own sake, you'll also be able to learn how to extend yourself a bit for maximal rewards.

CHAPTER 5

Strength Training

Be Strong, Not Wrong

Pumping iron? I know what you're thinking: a great idea if you want to be Mr. Universe, an Olympic lifter, or governor of California—but not in the cards for ordinary folks who just want to be healthy.

Until recently, most doctors would have agreed with you. Heavy-duty weight lifting narrows blood vessels and raises blood pressure, forcing the heart to pump against higher pressures. Many cardiologists were concerned that this could make the heart muscle thick and stiff and could lead to hypertension. Fortunately, new studies show that these concerns were unfounded, at least in the case of moderate strength training.

When done properly, strength training is actually good for the heart, circulation, and metabolism. But so is walking. Is there any need to add resistance exercise to a good CME program featuring walking or similar activities?

The answer is yes. Strength training is important, even for people who stay lean and fit with CME activities (see Chapter 4). There are two reasons for this—your muscles and your bones— and both are prime targets of the aging process.

Muscles get smaller and weaker as people age; it's a universal phenomenon that doctors call *sarcopenia*. You don't need a medical degree to see that sixty-year-olds are weaker and less muscular than twenty-year-olds. But you may be surprised to learn that muscle mass and strength begin to decline long before the changes are obvious. The loss of muscle typically begins at age thirty and progresses slowly thereafter. By age sixty, the changes are noticeable without any tests—and it's all downhill from there. In all, average thirty-year-olds can expect to lose about 25 percent of their muscle mass and strength by age seventy and another 25 percent by age ninety. That amounts to a loss of two to three pounds of muscle per decade, but the loss of muscle tissue does not usually cause a corresponding weight loss, since body fat tends to increase as muscle bulk declines.

Bones show a similar pattern. Bones undergo a constant process of remodeling throughout life as new tissue is formed and old bone is resorbed. In youth, bone formation has the upper hand; that's how kids grow. In young adulthood, the processes are balanced and bones are at their strongest. But beyond age forty, resorption outpaces bone formation; that's why older folks shrink. The loss of bone averages about 0.5 percent a year; in most men, the rate of loss is fairly steady, but in women it accelerates sharply at about the time of menopause. Doctors can detect bone loss by measuring the mineral density of bones. When the loss of bone density is mild, it's called *osteopenia*, when more severe, *osteoporosis*.

Weak muscles increase the risk of falls, and osteoporosis increases the risk of fractures, so it's easy to see why good health depends on strong muscles and bones. You can help by eating the right amount of protein for your muscles and by getting the right amount of calcium and vitamin D for your bones (see Chapter 12). Your doctor can help by testing bone density of postmenopausal women (and at-risk men) to see if medication is also needed. But even with diet and medication, you need to help yourself. Resistance exercises will build your muscles and bones. Weight-bearing exercises will also help your bones, as the force of gravity provides the healthful stress that stimulates bone formation.

Your body has more than six hundred muscles and two hundred bones—that's eight hundred reasons for considering strength training. And there's more. Strength training will improve your metabolism. Muscles burn calories faster than fat does, so as you gain muscle and lose fat, your metabolic rate will increase. Your muscle cells will become more responsive to insulin, so your blood sugar and insulin levels will decline, reducing your risk of diabetes.

Strength training is not as beneficial for cardiovascular health as CME activities, but it can help (see Table 5.1). Your cholesterol profile may improve, and, contrary to earlier beliefs, your heart function and blood pressure also stand to gain. In fact, a Harvard study of 44,452 men found that men who trained with weights for thirty or more minutes per week averaged a 23 percent lower risk of heart disease than men who did not use weights. And since strong muscles take pressure off joints, people with arthritis can often enjoy pain relief, particularly when they strengthen their quadriceps muscles for knee arthritis.

Strength training will help you look better and feel better. Your endurance and functional capacity will improve substantially.

TABLE 5.1 Comparing Exercises

It's not a question of either-or but both. CME and strength training are both important for health, and they complement each other nicely.

	CME	Strength Training
Improved heart function	+ + + +	+
Lower risk of heart attacks	+ + + +	+
Lower blood pressure	+ + +	+
Improved blood sugar levels	+ + +	+
Improved cholesterol levels	+ + +	+
Weight loss	+ + +	+
Muscular endurance	+	+ +
Muscle strength and power	+	+ + + +
Muscle mass	+	+ + + +
Bone calcium and strength		
(non–weight bearing)	+	
(weight bearing)	+ + +	

Even if you never hoist a barbell in competition, you'll feel the difference when you take out the trash, carry in the groceries, horse around with the kids, wrestle with a suitcase, or climb a flight of stairs. Best of all, perhaps, are the studies showing that for your health, if not your physique, moderate-intensity resistance training is as good as or better than high-intensity weight training.

When it comes to exercise, most Americans don't do what's good for them. That's particularly true of strength training. Older adults need it most but do it least. It's never too late to start. A landmark study of frail nursing home residents with an average age of eighty-seven found that modest resistance training produced an increase in muscle mass and strength, along with important functional gains in gait, stair-climbing, and spontaneous activity. And it's never too early to start either. A study of 6,089 Hawaiian men found that a good grip strength in midlife was linked to a reduced risk of disability and functional limitation in old age. In addition, Canadian researchers have reported that some aspects of muscular fitness and strength are associated with a reduced overall mortality rate.

When should you start strength training? How about now?

Getting Started

The American Heart Association now recommends strength training for cardiac patients as well as for healthy people. Still, you should pause to ask if resistance exercises are right for you.

Everyone should get a general checkup before embarking on a serious exercise program, and everyone should know how to spot signs of trouble (see Chapter 9). But lifting calls for a bit more care than walking. If you have heart disease that's causing symptoms or hypertension that's not well controlled, you should not begin strength training until your health has stabilized—and even then, get your doctor's clearance first. People with a moderate cardiac risk (see Chapter 3, Figures 3.1 and 3.2) should also get a physician's OK. And if you have back pain or other significant musculoskeletal problems, don't even bother to ask your doctor if you can lift until your pain has settled down (see Chapter 9 for tips on how to manage common musculoskeletal complaints).

Once you are ready to go, you'll have to decide what program is best for you. There are four basic approaches to strength training. You can use your body's own weight; you can use dumbbells, barbells, and ankle weights, which are known as free weights; you can use resistance machines, such as Cybex and Nautilus, at health clubs; or you can use elastic bands, which are often called stretchies. Needless to say, you can also combine these techniques or switch back and forth depending on factors such as time, travel, and the desire for a change.

Health clubs and gyms offer the ultimate opportunities for strength training (see Chapter 11). You can get an expert evaluation of your needs and personal instruction and supervision on resistance machines and free weights. But you can do very well on your own at home. For now, let's leave resistance machines to the pros and concentrate on a home program using free weights and your body's weight, with a few extra tips about elastic bands.

You'll need some equipment. For the body weight program, all you need is a sturdy, stable kitchen chair and a carpeted surface that will keep the chair from sliding; if you don't have a suitable carpet, place the chair against a wall for stability. For the free weight program, you'll need dumbbells and ankle weights.

Cast-iron dumbbells are inexpensive, and vinyl-coated weights are only slightly more costly. If you have problems with your hands, vinyl-coated or padded-grip dumbbells will be worth the extra cost. Health clubs have a wide range of weights for you to try, but it's not practical for most people to buy a whole set. To find out what weights you should buy, try out a few at a sporting goods or fitness store. For starters, pick a weight you can lift eight times in the military press or curl exercises (see "The Top Ten"). Since you'll progress to higher weights as you improve, you'll probably want to invest in another set two to three pounds heavier than the first and possibly a third set a few pounds heavier still. For example, many women will start with dumbbells of two, four, and six pounds, many men with pairs weighing four, six, and eight or ten pounds. For ankle weights, pick an adjustable set that will let you add a pound at a time until you reach ten (for women or older men) or twenty (for younger men and athletic women) pounds per leg. And while you're shopping, check out the elastic band sets to see if they appeal to you; because they are inexpensive and portable, they're good for travel, but if you use them heavily, they may stretch out and lose some benefit until you replace them.

Principles

Exercising for health means exercising regularly. In the case of CME activities, that means every day or nearly every day for moderate exercise or at least three or four times a week for intense or prolonged exercise. But strength training is different. To improve steadily without injury or undo soreness, your muscles need to recoup and recover after strength training. Any given exercise should be done in sets with one or two minutes of rest (or gentle stretching) between sets. In addition, you should schedule a full fifteen- to twenty-minute series of strength exercises only two to three times a week, always giving yourself at least forty-eight hours between sessions. Or if you prefer to devote just a few minutes a day to strength training, you can rotate your exercises so you don't stress the same major muscles groups on two consecutive days. Chapter 8 will offer model programs using both approaches.

High-repetition, low-resistance exercise is best. That means doing an exercise that does not seem difficult when it's performed once or twice but causes fatigue without exhaustion when it's repeated ten to fifteen times at a steady rhythm. As you improve, you'll be able to gradually increase the resistance until you reach a sustainable plateau. In general, each arm exercise should be performed in a set of ten to fifteen repetitions and each leg exercise in a set of eight to twelve reps. Do two or three sets of each exercise, giving yourself a one- or two-minute rest between sets.

Resistance training will strengthen only the specific muscles that are being exercised. That means constructing a program that exercises each of your major muscle groups in turn.

Warm up before and cool down after a training session. Five or ten minutes of stretching, light calisthenics, or walking is ideal.

Above all, use common sense and listen to your body. Most often, you'll hear sounds of harmony and improvement, but if you hear sounds of distress, you should back off and get help. Fatigue and mild muscle aches and stiffness usually resolve with rest and simple self-help measures, but chest pressure or pain, undue breathlessness, and light-headedness head the list of symptoms that warrant medical attention (see Chapter 9).

Don't do strength training if you are injured or ill. And when you resume exercise after a layoff, start slowly and work your way back gradually. In general, give yourself two days of reduced intensity for each day you miss due to illness or injury; you may be able to come back from layoffs caused by lack of diligence a bit more quickly.

Weight lifting requires special attention to technique. Start with weights that are comfortable. For some people it's as little as two to five pounds, for others it's ten to fifteen pounds or more, but it should never be more than 50 percent of the heaviest weight you can lift comfortably one time. Be sure your body mechanics are good. Keep your feet ten to twelve inches apart. Never lock your joints. Instead, keep your knees slightly bent and your back straight. Don't rock or sway. Move only the part of your body that you're trying to exercise. Don't jerk the weight. Lift slowly and smoothly, giving yourself three seconds to lift and another three to four seconds to return to your starting position. Breathe slowly and naturally. If possible, train yourself to exhale while you're lifting or pushing and inhale while you're lowering the weight. Never hold your breath. If you find yourself grunting with exertion, the weight is too heavy. Monitor your technique in a mirror or ask a friend to watch you.

The fifteen figures that follow outline a program that you can do at home with just a set of dumbbells and ankle weights and a sturdy chair—plus, of course, your body. If you choose to do the whole routine in a single session, start with the standing exercises, then move to the chair and finally the floor. Do each exercise eight to fifteen times, rest for a minute or two, then do a second set of eight to fifteen repetitions. Be sure to warm up before you start and cool down when you finish. And remember that your two or three weekly strength sessions should supplement, not replace, your daily CME activities. Try to get some CME activity nearly every day, but schedule your strength training on lighter CME days or on that occasional day off (see Chapter 8).

 ## The First Five

If you are not comfortable starting out with weights or if you are starting at a low level, you can use these five exercises to get started.

Squat

For your hips, thighs, and buttocks

Stand eight to twelve inches in front of a sturdy chair with your feet slightly more than shoulder width apart. Lean slightly forward from the waist. Keep your weight back on your heels, slowly lower yourself into a squatting position with your buttocks just touching the seat, and then slowly stand straight up. Give yourself about six seconds for each squat. Repeat eight to ten times for one set. When you are able to do this comfortably, add a second set after a one- to two-minute rest.

Wall Push-Up

For your shoulders, arms, and chest

Stand facing an empty wall, a little more than arm's length away. Lean forward, placing your palms flat on the wall at shoulder height and width. Keep your back straight as you bend your elbows and slowly lower your body toward the wall to a count of four, pause, and then slowly push yourself back upright. Repeat eight to ten times for one set. When you are able to do this comfortably, add a second set after a one- to two-minute rest.

Toe Stand

For your calves and ankles

Stand facing the back of a kitchen chair or countertop with your feet shoulder width apart. Using the chair or counter for balance, slowly lift yourself up on your toes to a count of four, pause, and then slowly lower yourself back down. Repeat eight to ten times for one set. When you are able to do this comfortably, add a second set after a one- to two-minute rest.

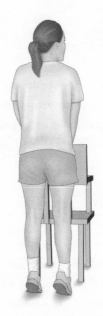

Chair Stand

For your abdomen and thighs

Place a pillow against the back of a
chair. Sit toward the front of the chair
with your knees bent and your feet
flat on the floor. Cross your arms on
your chest. Slowly lean back against
the pillow until you are in a
semireclining position. Pause, and
then raise your body forward until
you are sitting straight up. Slowly
stand up, using your hands as little
as possible. Pause and then sit down
again. Repeat eight to ten times for
one set. When you are able to do
this comfortably, add a second set
after a one- to two-minute rest.

Gripping

For your hands and wrists

Hold a tennis ball comfortably in your hand. Slowly squeeze it as hard as
you can, then slowly relax. Repeat eight to ten times, then switch to the
other hand and repeat for one set. When you are able to do this
comfortably, add a second set after a one- to two-minute rest.

The Top Ten

When it comes to exercise, one plan will not fit all. Although a
supervised individual exercise prescription is best, it's not always
available. Here is a set of ten basic exercises that can help most
people build strong bones and muscles. Start slowly and cautiously,
but build up steadily as you improve.

Military Press

For your arms, shoulders, and upper back

Stand with your feet slightly apart.
Hold a dumbbell in each hand at
shoulder height. With your palms
facing away from your body, slowly
lift upward until your arms are fully
extended, then slowly lower the
dumbbells to chest level. Repeat
eight to fifteen times. When you are
able to do this comfortably, add a
second set after a one- to two-
minute rest.

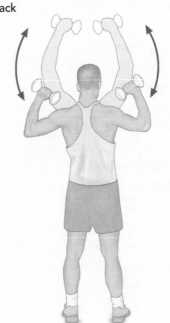

Lateral Raise

For your arms, shoulders, and upper back

With your feet slightly
apart, hold a dumbbell in
each hand with your palms
facing your thighs. Keeping
your arms straight, slowly
lift the dumbbells until they
are slightly above your
shoulders. Slowly lower the
dumbbells to your sides.
Repeat eight to fifteen
times. When you are able
to do this comfortably, add
a second set after a one- to
two-minute rest.

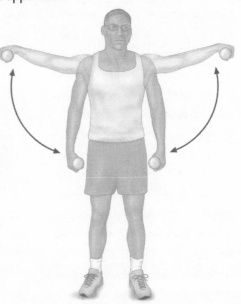

Upright Row

For your arms, shoulders, and upper back

Stand with your feet at
shoulder width. Hold a
dumbbell in each hand with
your palms facing your thighs.
Slowly lift the dumbbells to
shoulder level, keeping them
close together by allowing your
elbows to point outward.
Slowly lower the dumbbells to
your thighs. Repeat eight to
fifteen times. When you are
able to do this comfortably,
add a second set after a one-
to two-minute rest.

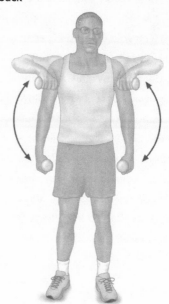

Curl

For your arms, shoulders, and upper back

Stand or sit comfortably with your
arms at your sides. Hold a dumbbell
in each hand, and slowly lift them to
the level of your upper chest,
keeping your arms close to your
sides. Lower the weights slowly, and
then repeat. Alternate the position of
your hands, first facing your palms
forward, then backward (reverse
curls). Repeat eight to fifteen times.
When you are able to do this
comfortably, add a second set after a
one- to two-minute rest.

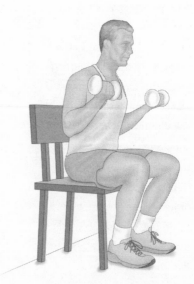

Partial Squat

For your hips and legs

Stand with your feet at shoulder
width. Hold a dumbbell in each hand
with your arms at your sides and your
palms facing inward. Slowly bend
your knees, lowering your buttocks
about eight inches while keeping
your arms down straight. Slowly rise
to an upright position. Repeat eight
to fifteen times. When you are able
to do this comfortably, add a second
set after a one- to two-minute rest.

Hip Extension

For your hips and legs

Wearing ankle weights, stand eight inches
behind a sturdy chair. Using the back of the
chair for balance, bend your trunk forward
forty-five degrees, and then extend
your right leg straight behind you.
Slowly lower your foot to the
floor. Repeat with each
leg eight to fifteen
times. When you are
able to do this
comfortably, add a
second set after a one-
to two-minute rest.

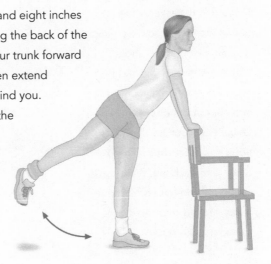

Lateral Leg Raise

For your hips and legs

Wearing ankle weights, stand behind a sturdy chair, using the back for balance. Slowly raise your right leg to the side until your foot is eight inches off the floor. Keeping your knee straight, slowly lower your foot to the floor. Repeat with each leg eight to fifteen times. When you are able to do this comfortably, add a second set after a one- to two-minute rest.

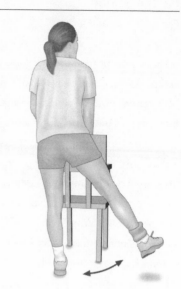

Knee Extension

For your hips and legs

Wearing ankle weights, sit in a firm straight-backed chair with your knees six inches apart and a small towel folded under your lower thighs. Slowly lift your right foot until your leg is straight out in front of you. Lower your foot slowly to the floor. Repeat eight to fifteen times with each leg. When you are able to do this comfortably, add a second set after a one- to two-minute rest.

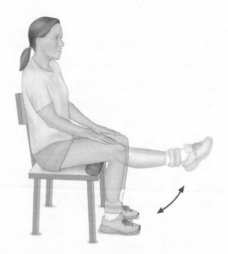

Heel Raise and Dip

For your hips and legs

Stand on the bottom step of a staircase, holding on to the handrail for balance. Place the balls of your feet on the first step, with your heels projecting out. Slowly raise your heels, shifting your weight to your toes. Slowly lower your heels as far as you can, shifting your weight to your heels. Return to the starting position. Repeat eight to fifteen times. When you are able to do this comfortably, add a second set after a one- to two-minute rest.

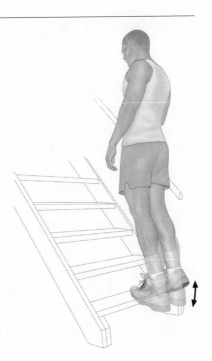

Bent-Knee Sit-Up

For your abdomen and trunk

Lie on your back with your knees bent, your feet flat on the floor or mat, and your arms folded across your chest. Raise your torso until your elbows touch your knees. Slowly lower yourself to the floor. Repeat eight to fifteen times. When you are able to do this comfortably, add a second set after a one- to two-minute rest.

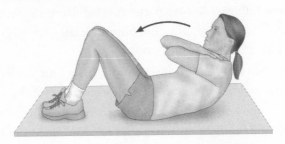

Moving On

Strength training is most effective when your muscles are contracting against a force slightly stronger than they are used to encountering. When you are able to do two sets of lifts with your starting weights, you are ready to move on to heavier weights. But before you do, be sure that you are strong enough to complete the second set without cutting corners by speeding up your lift, lengthening your pauses excessively, or allowing your form and technique to deteriorate. You should be tired but not worn out at the end of your workout. If you are exhausted, use lighter weights until you catch up with yourself. But if you feel you could go on without any problems, it's time to jack up your weight. That means adding half- or one-pound weights to each ankle weight and switching to dumbbells that are one to three pounds heavier. Until you are used to the heavier weights, though, do your first set with your old ankle weights or dumbbells, and then switch to the heavier ones.

 ## Pumping Rubber

If you do a lot of traveling, have extremely limited storage space at home, or simply don't cotton to weights, consider using elastic bands for your strength training. Physical therapists have been using them for years to help patients rehab from injuries or operations, and "stretchies" are now commercially available in inexpensive kits.

Resistance bands are nothing more than simple rubber tubes with plastic handles and/or door anchors attached at the ends. Like dumbbells, they come in various levels of resistance, so you can start light and move up as you progress. And since the resistance increases as you stretch the band, you can start out with a partial stretch and then lengthen it to intensify your workout.

If you use elastic bands, follow the same principles that govern dumbbells. That means warming up and cooling down, doing sets, giving your muscles time to recover between workouts, and starting modestly but advancing steadily as you improve. You can strengthen the same muscles with bands that you can with dumbbells, if you use good form and follow the directions that come with each set of plastic bands.

Pump rubber, pump iron, lift your body, or use resistance machines at a gym. The choice is yours, and the rewards will be yours, too. By any method, lifting will give you a lift.

CHAPTER 6

Flexibility Training

Stretching for Health

t won't improve your heart or lower your cholesterol like walking or swimming. It can't slim you down or lower your risk of diabetes like biking or jogging. It may not lower your blood pressure as well as skating or dancing, and it can't compete with strength training to build up your muscles and bones. It may not make you slimmer, faster, or stronger, but it's worth a significant portion of the time you set aside for exercise. It's *flexibility training*—stretching.

 Flexibility and Stability

People sometimes liken the human skeleton to the steel girders that support tall buildings. It's a reasonable analogy, but it has limits. True, your bones are strong and stiff, and they are at least as important and complicated as a bunch of beams. But your skeleton does more than hold your body up. It also allows you to bend and twist, to move. That movement requires flexibility.

FIGURE 6.1 The Knee Joint

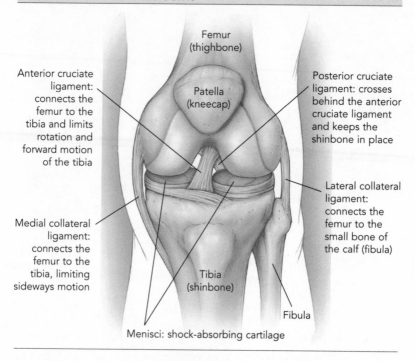

Femur (thighbone)

Anterior cruciate ligament: connects the femur to the tibia and limits rotation and forward motion of the tibia

Patella (kneecap)

Posterior cruciate ligament: crosses behind the anterior cruciate ligament and keeps the shinbone in place

Lateral collateral ligament: connects the femur to the small bone of the calf (fibula)

Medial collateral ligament: connects the femur to the tibia, limiting sideways motion

Tibia (shinbone)

Fibula

Menisci: shock-absorbing cartilage

Your bones meet at your joints, and that's where movement takes place. Your body has dozens of joints, each with a special structure and role (see Figure 6.1). Despite their differences, some fundamental things apply to nearly every one. The ends of the bones that meet at a joint are covered with smooth, slippery tissues called *cartilage*, which allows the bones to slide easily without damaging each other. A typical joint is surrounded by a capsule of *fibrous tissue* filled with *synovial fluid*, which cushions the joints and provides nutrition for the cartilage. This is a crucial task, since cartilage does not have any blood supply of its own and can't get oxygen and nutrients any other way.

Joints are designed for flexibility, but they must also be strong. They are held together by *ligaments*, sturdy bands of fibrous tissue that run across joints, connecting bone to bone (see Figure 6.1). Strength and stability are also provided by muscles and their *tendons*, the fibrous bands that connect muscles to bones. When a muscle contracts, it shortens, which pulls on the tendon and moves the bone around its joint.

Like personality, flexibility varies from person to person: some folks are loose, others tight. On average, women are more flexible than men. And within any one body, flexibility varies from joint to joint. In general, joints that are habitually moved through their full range of motion are more flexible than those that are not put to work on a regular basis; it's "resting is rusting" redux. Flexibility also varies from left to right. It's not the body politic at work, but the body's natural tendency toward right- or left-handedness. Because muscles get stronger (and tighter!) with use, right-handed people tend to be stronger but less flexible on the right, left-handed folks the reverse. Finally, flexibility varies with age. Young people are more flexible in their bodies as well as in their ability to adapt to social changes, but aging brings stiff bodies and, often, rigid habits and opinions.

All this might suggest that flexibility is a gift of nature, stiffness a fact of life. Fortunately, that's not entirely true. Like cardiovascular function, body fat, and muscular strength, flexibility can be improved substantially with training.

 Loosen Up

Healthy joints are both flexible and stable, but the two don't always go together. It's all too easy to sacrifice flexibility for stability—and that's where stretching comes in.

Each joint has a natural limit to its mobility. If a joint is forced beyond its normal *range of motion*, it will place abnormal stress on tissues. That's why a misstep can injure your ankle—the excessive force stretches ligaments, producing a *sprain*. When muscles and tendons are stressed and stretched, the injury is called a *strain* (see Chapter 9).

Abnormal stretching is not a good thing, but neither is excessive stiffness. When muscles become stronger, they tend to become shorter and tighter. Tendons, too, get stiffer as they get shorter;

that's why exercises as different as weight training and running can make you stiff. And because elastic tissue loses spring and resiliency with age, the mere passage of time will also make you stiff. The good news, though, is that you can fight back; stretching exercises may not restore the limberness of youth, but they can certainly help.

Why Stretch?

There are four reasons to stretch: improved physical functioning, a better sense of well-being, a reduced risk of injury, and an improved mental outlook.

You'll be able to see for yourself that stretching can improve physical functioning. Because you'll stand taller and move more gracefully, you'll look better. Daily activities as simple as bending down to pick up a newspaper will be easier, so you'll feel better. Stretching will also help you feel less sore after a day of golf or gardening. Your balance will improve, reducing the risk of the falls that can be so devastating (see Chapter 7). And as your body functions more efficiently, you'll gain self-confidence and a sense of well-being.

Feeling better is one thing; being healthier is another. Improved functioning would be reason enough to stretch, but virtually all physical therapists, trainers, and coaches are quick to give you a second reason: a reduced risk of injury. A widely quoted 2004 study, however, has cast doubt on that purported benefit.

The study was performed by a team of four scientists from the Centers for Disease Control and Prevention. They conducted a computerized search of the world's medical literature and iden-tified 361 investigations of stretching and health. However, only six of these studies met modern scientific standards for validity, and the new report is based on a meta-analysis of these few tri-als. It concluded that "there is not sufficient evidence to endorse or discontinue routine stretching before or after exercise to prevent injury among competitive or recreational athletes. Further research, especially well-conducted randomized clinical trials, is urgently needed."

Many press reports summarized the research with headlines to the effect that stretching does not work. That's not accurate. In fact, the study concluded that there are not enough data to draw any firm conclusion. I agree, but a look at the meta-analysis itself raises additional considerations. The subjects in all six experiments were healthy, active young men, either football players or military recruits. Twenty-something guys are usually quite flexible, so it's no surprise that stretching appeared to add little benefit. Let's await research on fifty- and sixty-something folks before we come to any conclusions.

Throughout this book, I've tried to base my recommendations on current scientific evidence. On the few occasions when I use clinical and personal experience to give advice, I'll let you know. And this is one such situation. Until there is good evidence to the contrary, I'll stick with the belief that regular stretching can reduce the risk of injury. Conventional wisdom is . . . wise.

In any case, there is a final reason to stretch: to reduce mental tension and promote relaxation. It's another recommendation based on traditional wisdom, but in this case, the tradition dates far beyond the locker room, all the way to ancient India, where the practice of yoga originated.

Many of the stretching exercises I'll recommend later in this chapter are based on the less-demanding postures (called *asanas*) of hatha yoga, the form that is most popular in the United States today. Hatha yoga also involves disciplined breathing and meditation. But even without these elements, stretching itself can help relieve tension; as your muscles relax, so will your mind. In fact, a modern method of stress reduction uses progressive muscular relaxation without the stretching to improve mental health.

Stretch before and after exercise to warm up, cool down, and (I think) reduce your risk of injury. And consider a little stretching when you are tense and uptight. Many people find that a few minutes of stretching first thing in the morning helps start the day well and that a few minutes at bedtime promotes peaceful sleep. If you agree, try standing up from your desk for a little discreet stretching when you're tense, and use a similar approach to take the edge off travel, which is edgy enough in our modern world.

Stretch for health. It's the smart thing to do.

Stretching Facts

Like strength and endurance, limberness varies from person to person. Flexibility also varies in the different parts of your body. Joggers, for example, are notoriously stiff in their hamstrings; paradoxically, perhaps, people who sit behind a desk all day are prone to the same problem. Concentrate on the muscles you use most and the joints that are least flexible, but don't neglect the other parts of your body. Above all, give yourself time to improve. Restoring lost flexibility is a slow process. If you are impatient and push too hard, you'll produce the very injury you want to avoid. Be patient but persistent. Establish realistic goals. If you are stiffer than average, you may never get to a full range of motion, but you can surely make progress. Finally, don't try to improve on human nature; there is no benefit to being "double-jointed," and there is no point in trying to stretch beyond a joint's normal range of motion.

Stretching is a time-honored practice, and various methods have evolved over time. One technique is passive stretching. It's well named, since it doesn't require any effort on the part of the person who is being stretched. Instead, a partner moves the target joint through a range of motion to produce slow, gentle muscle lengthening and joint motion. Passive stretching is favored by many physical therapists during the early phases of rehabilitation from an injury or operation.

Dynamic, or ballistic, stretching is just the reverse. It involves rapidly lengthening muscles by active bouncing movements based on calisthenics. Once very popular, dynamic stretching is now discouraged because of the risk of injury. Active calisthenics can provide some benefits of dynamic stretching, but it should be preceded by static stretching (described shortly) and warming-up activities. Even so, dynamic stretching is not a good idea for people who are stiff or tight, the very people who most need flexibility training.

The most sophisticated form of stretching is proprioceptive neuromuscular facilitation (PNF), also in the realm of physical therapy. First, the patient voluntarily contracts the muscle group that works against the muscles to be stretched. Next, the therapist gradually stretches the patient by passively forcing motion and muscle lengthening. PNF is designed to train nerves and muscles to work together smoothly, as well as to stretch out muscles and joints.

The most popular and widely recommended stretching technique is static stretching, which is based on yoga. It is simply slow, sustained muscle lengthening that you initiate and control on your own. Simple or not, good technique is important to get improvement without injury.

The goal of static stretching is to establish a posture and then use the weight of your body to stretch your tissues. But the stretch must always be gentle and gradual—you should be able to feel a mild pull on your muscles, tendons, and ligaments, but it should never be painful. Don't bounce or jerk your body into position; instead, exert force slowly and steadily. And although your stretches will often aim to straighten out your limbs, you should never lock them in a fully straight position; instead, maintain a little bend in your joints as you stretch.

If you are just starting out, don't try to hold any stretch for more than ten to fifteen seconds. As you improve, build up gradually to twenty to thirty seconds. Give yourself plenty of time to improve. As your tissues gain flexibility, you'll be able to stretch longer without pain or fatigue. Start out with a deep breath, and let it out slowly as you stretch. Focus your mind on the part of your body that's being stretched. Relax your body, mind, and breathing after each stretch, wait for fifteen to thirty seconds before repeating the stretch, and then move on to another part of your body. Don't be surprised if one side of your body is stiffer than the other; most people have a dominant side, which becomes stronger but also tighter with extra use over the years.

 ## A Basic Routine

If you have special needs, you'll benefit from individual instruction and supervision. A physical therapist, a good personal trainer, or an experienced yoga teacher can design an individual routine for people who need extra help and can also plan advanced stretching for people who are ready to move on.

Average people can use a balanced program like the following ten basic stretching exercises. If you are starting on your own, try to have a friend or relative watch you to be sure your positions and angles are right. Start with standing stretches, then sit on an exercise mat or a thick towel or rug for your floor exercises. Save your back for last.

Shoulder Blade Scratch

For your shoulder muscles, rotator cuff, and upper back

Reach back and down with one arm as if to scratch your opposite shoulder blade. Reach up with your other arm, trying to clasp your hands behind your back. If you can't make the connection, use a towel to bridge the gap. Gradually pull up on your lower arm, gently stretching your shoulder. Relax and then repeat before reversing your arm position to stretch your other side.

Towel Stretch

For your triceps, shoulders, and upper back

Roll up a towel and grasp it between your hands in front of you. Keeping your arms straight, lift the towel over your head and then as far back as you can.

Wall Lean

For your calves and Achilles tendons

Stand about three feet from a wall, with your feet pointing straight ahead. Step forward with one foot, but keep your back knee straight. Push your pelvis forward as far as comfortable, keeping your heels firmly on the floor. As you improve, start farther from the wall to give yourself a greater stretch; aim to bring your leg to a forty-five-degree angle with the floor. Relax and then repeat with your rear knee bent to move the stretch down to your Achilles tendon. Relax again and then switch to the other side.

Hamstring Stretch

For your hamstrings

Rest one heel on the second or
third step of a staircase. Keep your
knees straight as you lean forward
to touch the foot on the step. Keep
your head down and your pelvis as
far forward as possible. Relax and
then repeat before switching to the
other side. As you improve, you'll
be able to reach your toes instead
of just your ankle. Then you can
move up to a higher step.

Thigh Stretch

For your quadriceps muscles

Stand facing a wall, close enough
to touch it for balance if necessary.
Keep one leg straight while you
bend your other knee and grasp
your ankle to pull your heel up
toward your buttocks. Relax and
then repeat before switching to the
other side.

Hip Stretch

For your hip muscles

Sit on the floor with your legs spread to the sides. Bend one knee, point your foot toward your other leg, grasp your ankle, and lift your leg upward. Relax and then repeat before switching to the other side.

Groin Stretch

For your groin muscles

Sit on the floor with the soles of your feet together and your knees bent out to the sides. Place your forearms on the inside of your knees, and gradually press down toward the floor. Relax and then repeat. As you improve, start with your heels closer to your body. If you are able to lean forward as you stretch your groin, you'll also stretch your lower back.

Starter's Stretch

For your groin and thighs

Get in a sprinter's starting position, with your rear knee on the floor and your front foot flat on the floor. Place your hands at the sides of your front foot. Gradually straighten your back knee as you lift up on your toes and bend forward. Relax and then repeat before switching to the other side.

William's Stretch

For your lower back

Lie on your back with your legs straight out on the floor. Bring one knee up to your chest, pulling it in with your hands as you curl your head toward your knee. Relax and then repeat before switching to the other side. As you improve, you can bring both knees up together.

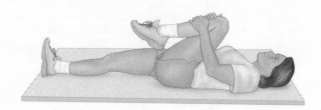

Cat Stretch

For your upper back and shoulders

Rest on your knees, then lower your head and reach forward with one arm and then the other (both arms will be stretched out in front of you). Relax and then repeat.

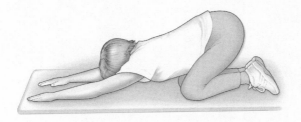

 # Flexibility First—and Last

A basic stretching routine should take you about ten to fifteen minutes. That makes it an ideal way to warm up before you play a sport or go for a brisk walk. It's also the best way to cool down afterward. And remember that stretching can be just as beneficial for working in the garden or making household repairs as it is for playing golf or tennis.

In an ideal world, you'd go through the whole basic stretching routine every day. If that doesn't fit into your real world, you can still get lots of benefit from fitting in a few minutes to stretch whenever you can. Chapter 8 will illustrate model programs that include flexibility training. Look it over, then figure out what's best for you, always remembering to put extra work into the parts of your body that most need flexibility training.

When it comes to preventing exercise-induced injuries, stretching is a means to an end, but it can also be a goal of its own. Many people stretch in the morning, others before bed. Try it to limber up after a long car trip or during a long flight. Perhaps stretching will help you relax when you are under stress. If you are flexible and creative about when you stretch, your body will stay limber and your mind may become more relaxed. It is not much of a stretch to say that it's a big return for a small investment.

CHAPTER 7

Exercises for Balance

Stand Tall, Don't Fall

Most exercise programs, even those that are fair and balanced, don't say a word about exercise for balance. Indeed, balance plays no role in preventing heart disease, hypertension, stroke, obesity, diabetes, cancer, or the other major woes that respond to CME activities. Still, balance is important for health. A good sense of balance will greatly reduce your risk of falling, and a special set of exercises can help keep you on your toes.

Falls are usually classified as accidents, not illnesses. Like so many accidents, though, most falls are predictable and preventable. The trick is to keep your body stable and strong, to reduce environmental hazards (discussed a little later in this chapter), and to use common sense. And before you dismiss the health impact of falling, consider that falls are responsible for most of the three hundred thousand hip fractures in the United States each year. Even worse, about sixteen thousand Americans die from falls annually—more than the number of Americans who die in fires, from drowning, and as a result of firearm accidents combined.

 ## Normal Gait and Balance

Although all healthy people develop a sense of balance and a stable gait without instruction, most will benefit from exercises designed to maintain these natural abilities throughout the aging process.

Stand on Your Own Two Feet

It's easy to take the upright posture for granted; most children learn to stand and walk between twelve and eighteen months of age, and from then on the upright stance is a defining characteristic of humanity. But although standing and walking are natural and automatic, they are highly complex tasks that require the coordinated interaction of many of the body's organ systems. Balance is a big achievement.

To stand up and stay up, the body must access its orientation in space. Specialized nerve cells called *proprioceptors* work continuously to provide crucial information to the brain. No less important are visual input and the sense of equilibrium that relies on the *vestibular apparatus* of the inner ear. The spinal cord and brain coordinate all this information, but the nervous system can't defy gravity on its own. Instead, it sends signals to the muscles of the limbs and trunk, calling on them to contract or relax as needed. Last but not least, the heart and circulation must also be able to thwart gravity by maintaining the blood pressure when people stand, so the brain can get the blood it needs to keep up its good work.

Things Change

It takes babies a year or so to develop the capacity to walk and another year to develop a stable gait. The sense of balance continues to improve during the early childhood years. Unless illness or injury interferes, people should retain postural stability and a secure gait throughout life. But with advancing age, things change. Reflexes and reaction times slow, and it also takes more time for the vestibular apparatus to adjust to changes in posture. Vision tends to dim, and muscle strength declines. All this is normal, and healthy bodies make adjustments to compensate. As people enter their sixties and seventies, they tend to walk with a shorter, broader stride, and they don't lift their feet as high when they take a step. Older people typically stoop forward when they walk; they hold their arms slightly flexed and don't swing their arms as far as they used to. On average, the speed of walking slows by 10 to 20 percent. The sense of balance also declines over the years, in no small part due to muscle weakness, stiffness, and inactivity. When it comes to balance, practice won't make perfect, but it sure will help.

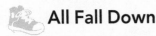 ## All Fall Down

The mature stance and gait may not be a change for the better, but they work quite well. Still, it doesn't take much to bring a person down to earth. Illness, medications, or sedentary living can undo the successful adaptations that keep older people upright. Add environmental hazards as simple as a loose rug or missing handrail, and you've got the perfect formula for a fall.

Although falls are hardly restricted to senior citizens, they become progressively more common as people age. One of every three sixty-five-year-olds will fall in the course of a single year; by age eighty, a person's chance of falling during a year is 50 percent. In about half of all falls, pride is the only casualty, but mild to moderate injuries occur in 40 percent, and 10 percent result in fractures and other serious injuries. All in all, falls cost the U.S. economy some $20 billion each year.

Accidents are chance events, random and unforeseeable. But most falls are not accidents in the truest sense of the word. In fact, most falls are predictable, potentially serious events just waiting to happen. Here are some of the things that increase a person's risk of falling:

- **Age.** The older you are, the greater your risk—unless you take the preventive steps that have been proven effective (see later in this chapter).
- **Inactivity.** The boys in the locker room were right after all: use it or lose it. When muscles are not exercised, they *atrophy*, losing bulk and strength. Inactivity also slows the reflexes. As a result, it's hard for sedentary people to stop a slip before it becomes a fall.
- **Illness.** Neurological illnesses, such as Parkinson's disease and strokes, are obvious risk factors. Not so obvious are diabetes and cardiovascular disease, but they can make people dizzy and unstable when they stand. Falling blood pressure (*orthostatic hypotension*) is the usual culprit. And a 2000 study reminds us that a large meal can increase the risk of orthostatic hypotension, particularly in older people taking blood pressure medication.
- **Medication.** Sedatives and antidepressants head the list; by blunting the senses, they increase the risk of falls. Contrary to hopes and expectations, the newer *selective serotonin reuptake inhibitor* (SSRI) *antidepressants* in the Prozac family are no safer than the older *tricyclic* drugs in the Elavil family, at least when it comes to falling.
- **Hospitalization.** Patients who are hospitalized for any medical problem are almost always subject to three major risk factors: illness, inactivity, and medication. It's no surprise, then, that a 2000 study found that the risk of falling quadruples during the first two weeks after a patient is discharged from the hospital—and that 15 percent of all rehospitalizations are caused by falls.
- **Alcohol.** Although it's often overlooked in older people, alcohol is an important contributor to falls. Just a drink or two can impair balance, coordination, and judgment enough

to turn a stumble into a headlong fall. In fact, all the things that can impair people's ability to drive can also increase their risk of falling.

- **Poor vision.** If you can't see where you're going, you may find yourself going down.
- **Environmental hazards.** External problems trigger about half of all falls. Icy streets, wet floors, and errant banana peels are among the classic examples, but a loose rug or trailing telephone cord are even more likely to trip you up.
- **Poor judgment.** If you never climb a ladder, you'll never fall from one. If you walk on a treadmill or at the mall instead of outside when it's icy, you'll reduce your chances of slipping and falling.

 ## Are You Out of Balance?

Although prevention is for everyone, people at high risk may need special help. For example, although physical activity should be part of everyone's daily routine, some people will benefit from special exercises for balance. Review the result of your balance self-assessment test from Chapter 3 to see how you compare to others of your age and gender. And here are additional ways to test your stability:

- Stand up from a firm chair without using your hands.
- Stand with your feet together and your eyes closed.
- Walk and talk simultaneously.
- Walk a straight line, putting your feet right in front of each other as if you were on a tightrope.
- Brush your teeth while standing on one foot.

Although these tasks sound easy, they may be harder than you think, so be careful when you test yourself. And if your results suggest that you may be on shaky ground, ask your doctor to check your gait and balance, the sensation in your feet, and your blood pressure when you stand up quickly. If you have specific problem areas, neurologists or physical therapists may be able to help.

Above all, though, do some simple exercises to help yourself. It is true that some of the drastic age-related decline in balance displayed in Table 3.8 is an inevitable consequence of human biology, but much of it is the result of human behavior. In this case, the behavior is sitting around instead of moving around; for your sense of balance, as for your health in general, disuse is abuse.

Your Balancing Act

If your sense of balance is good, you can keep it that way simply by exercising for general health. That means a good foundation of CME activity; walking and climbing stairs are particularly important for balance. Activities such as biking and skating call for good balance, and people who continue enjoying these pursuits throughout life will help retain the equilibrium of youth. Sports like tennis and basketball require footwork and coordination, which will also help. Over time, it's true, many people switch from these "kids' games" to golf. That's fine for health if you walk the course. A 2004 study showed that elderly golfers had much better balance than their healthy but sedentary peers. In fact, the golfers were as stable as age-matched Tai Chi practitioners, and both were on a par with much younger subjects.

Strength and flexibility training will also help. The partial squat, lateral leg raise, knee exension, and hip extension, as illustrated in Chapter 5, are particularly important for keeping your legs strong. Many of the exercises in this chapter will keep your lower body limber.

Here are some exercises that will improve your sense of balance. If you need more help, consider group classes and/or physical therapy.

Toe Stand

Stand up straight, holding on to a counter or to the back of a sturdy chair for balance. Raise yourself onto your toes and stay there for five to ten seconds before lowering yourself. Repeat five to ten times for one set. Rest and then do another set. As you improve, touch the chair or counter with only one finger, then without using your hands. After you've mastered this, try the exercise with your eyes closed.

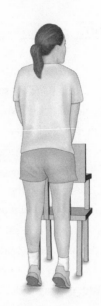

Hip Flexion

Stand about two feet from a wall so you can reach out to touch it with your hand for support if necessary. Slowly lift one leg (bent at the knee) off the floor and raise it until your thigh is nearly parallel to the floor. Hold it there for five to ten seconds, then slowly lower it. Pause and then repeat five to ten times for one set. Rest and then do another set. Switch to your other leg and repeat. As you improve, touch the wall with only one finger, then do the exercise without touching the wall. After you've mastered this, try the exercise with your eyes closed.

Toe Point

Stand about two feet from a wall so you can use your hand for support if necessary. Keeping both knees straight, lift one leg forward until your toe points thirty to forty-five degrees upward. Hold the position for five to ten seconds, then slowly lower your leg. Rest and then repeat five to ten times for one set. Switch to your other leg and repeat. When you have mastered this, try the exercise with your eyes closed.

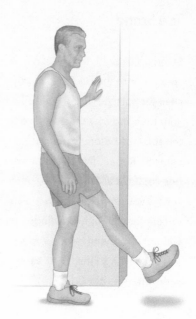

Hip Extension

Stand twelve to eighteen inches from a counter or the back of a sturdy chair. Bend forward at your hips to a forty-five-degree angle, holding on to the chair for balance. Slowly lift one leg backward without bending your knee, pointing your toes, or leaning your chest any farther forward. Hold for five to ten seconds, then slowly return to your starting position. Repeat five to ten times for one set. Rest and then do another set. Switch to your other leg and then repeat. As you improve, use only one fingertip for support, then do the exercise without using your hands. After you've mastered this, try the exercise with your eyes closed.

Lateral Raise

Stand up straight, holding on to a countertop or the back of a sturdy chair. Slowly lift one leg ten to twelve inches out to the side, keeping your back and both legs straight. Hold for five to ten seconds, then slowly lower your leg. Pause and then repeat five to ten times for one set. Rest and then do another set. Switch to your other leg and repeat. As you improve, use only one fingertip for support, then do the exercise without using your hands. After you've mastered this, try the exercise with your eyes closed.

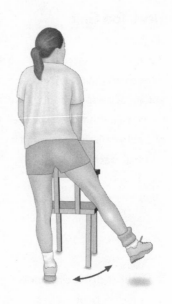

One-Legged Stance

Balance on one foot while you bend your other leg up at the knee. Hold for five to ten seconds, then relax. Repeat five to ten times, then switch to the other leg. At first you may need to touch a wall for balance, but as you improve you may be able to keep your arms out in front of you. And as you progress, try to maintain the one-legged stance for longer periods of time. Your goal should be one to two minutes on each leg, first in shorter segments that are repeated, and eventually in one to three continuous periods.

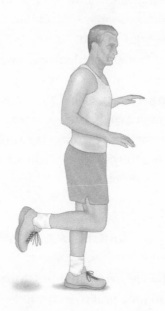

Heel-Toe Gait

Practice heel-to-toe walking as if you were on a tightrope. Hold your arms out at your sides or touch a wall for balance if necessary. Walk the length of a long hallway, then turn around and walk back.

If you do these exercises as a single block, schedule them at least three times a week on days between your strength training (see Chapter 8). Remember, too, that you can do many similar things anywhere, anytime during daily life. Practice standing on one foot while brushing your teeth, talking on the phone, or waiting for the bus. Sit down in your chair and get up from it without using your hands. Act like a kid, walking heel to toe along straight lines; you may look childish, but a youthful sense of balance will be your reward.

If you find these exercises daunting, a physical therapist or an experienced trainer can give you individual help. In addition, many health clubs, Ys, and senior centers offer exercise classes that emphasize balance training. Wobble-board, balance-beam, and trampoline exercises are available for advanced work, as are dance programs. And if group activities are your thing, consider taking a tai chi class.

Tai Chi: An Answer from the East

Tai chi originated in China about seven hundred years ago. Its philosophical roots lie in the Taoist principle that a life force called chi is responsible for health. According to the belief, chi can be bolstered through a program that combines deep breathing, mental relaxation, and a series of slow, graceful body movements that flow into each other.

The movements of tai chi are slow and flowing in the manner of a stately dance. About 108 movements are available to the practitioner, who selects a series and performs the movements continuously while standing over a thirty-minute period. The maneuvers were originally designed to mimic animal movements, such as those of a white crane or snake. Some are easy, others difficult; all require instruction, practice, and concentration.

Tai chi promotes balance, coordination, body stability, and body awareness. Modern scientific studies in the United States show that people who take up tai chi can develop better balance in just twelve weeks; even more important, they enjoy as much as a 50 percent lower risk of falling. And these gentle forms of moderate exercise can also help lower blood pressure and improve cardiovascular conditioning. Devotees also report psychosocial benefits, but these have not been scientifically evaluated.

Tai chi is not for everyone. But even if this Asian tradition is not your cup of tea, it shows how exercise can improve balance and health.

A Balanced Program

Exercise is the key to better balance. But if you are at risk of falling, you should also take some simple practical steps to help prevent that "accident" from happening:

- Get enough calcium and vitamin D to prevent osteoporosis. Then even if you bend, you won't be as likely to break (see Chapter 12).
- Have your eyes checked regularly. If you need corrective lenses, wear them regularly even when you're "just" walking around your house. But never wear reading glasses when you're up and about.

- Review your medications with your doctor. Older people often need medications, but some of them can backfire, increasing the risk of falls and injuries. Use tranquilizers, sleeping pills, and antidepressants only when you really need them, and work with your doctor to find the gentlest medication and the lowest effective dose.
- If you choose to use alcohol, drink responsibly and moderately. Be particularly careful if you take medications that can be sedating.
- Have your blood pressure checked when you are lying and standing, especially if you have diabetes or take blood pressure pills. If your blood pressure falls when you stand or if getting up makes you light-headed or dizzy, you should always be sure to get up slowly, dangling your feet on the floor before you get out of bed.
- Keep your footing. Keep your feet healthy and wear the right footgear. Never wear shoes or slippers that are loose or untied. Don't wear shoes with shiny, slippery soles or with thick rubber soles that can catch on carpets. Flat shoes with a wide, thin sole will give you the best feel of the floor and the greatest stability.
- If you need a cane or another assistive device, use it.

Household precautions are also important. More than half of all falls occur at home. Don't let your castle trip you up. Follow these guidelines:

- Make sure you have good lighting, especially at night. Use a night-light in your bathroom, hallway, and bedroom.
- Avoid high-gloss floor waxes, glossy paint, and other slippery surfaces. If you spill something, dry it up promptly.
- Avoid loose area rugs; tack down the edges of room rugs.
- Avoid clutter and loose objects, including electric wires and telephone cords.

- Be sure your stairs have secure handrails on both sides as well as nonslip treads or closely woven carpeting. Good lighting is particularly important on stairways.
- Place nonslip mats in tubs and showers; they can also be helpful near sinks and washing machines. Consider installing handrails in your bathroom if you are at risk for falling.
- Organize your closets and pantry so you don't have to use a stepladder or stool.
- Move furniture out of heavily trafficked areas. Don't sleep on a bed that's too high. Don't sit on chairs that are unstable or too low.
- Pay attention. Watch your step, particularly on stairs. Don't dash to answer the phone or door. Don't carry objects that are too heavy or too bulky for you.

Be just as careful away from home, particularly in wet or wintry weather.

Like other accidents, most falls can be prevented. Don't overlook effective precautions just because they seem so simple. Follow the advice that Shakespeare gives in *Henry IV*, Part I: "Out of this nettle, danger, we pluck this flower, safety."

Exercise for balance, and construct a balanced program to prevent falls. It's the upright thing to do.

CHAPTER 8

Constructing Your Program

The No Sweat Exercise Pyramids

t really does sound like a lot: exercises for your heart and metabolism, for strength, for flexibility, and for balance. Life is busy, the days are short. Perhaps tomorrow . . .

Time is limited and there is a lot to do. But the beauty of moderate exercise is that you can fit it into your life—and the importance of moderate exercise means that you should fit it in for your life.

To make exercise work for you, construct a program that's right for your unique situation. Consider your needs and goals, your abilities and experience, your likes and dislikes, your resources and commitments. Above all, consider your health, both today and in the years ahead.

Although each of us will construct a unique program, and each program will change over time, all of us have certain fundamental concerns in common. To address these concerns, I'll offer four model programs for you to consider. Each model program will be displayed in its own exercise pyramid that will show you how the pieces you need can fit together into a program that will keep you healthy. Because of its wide applicability, we'll spend most time on the basic pyramid and companion training schedule. Finally, we'll consider common obstacles to success—and how you can overcome them.

The No Sweat Basic Pyramid

The basic pyramid has six building blocks and an optional component (see Figure 8.1).

You may be surprised to see that nutrition occupies the base of the pyramid. Eating, it's true, is not a form of exercise, even for the most voracious among us. Remember, though, that this Harvard guide is a health book first and foremost. Good nutrition and regular exercise are equal, indispensable partners in the effort to prevent disease and enhance health. Competitive athletes may have a few special dietary needs, but for most of us, the basics will do very nicely. Chapter 12 will review these basics.

CME deserves its position on the next layer of the pyramid. Along with a good diet, CME is the way to gain important protection from many of the medical woes that ravage too many of us, including heart disease, hypertension, stroke, diabetes, obesity, and certain common malignancies. Fortunately, you can get all these benefits without pushing yourself—but if you use the No Sweat approach to exercise for health, you'll have to exercise nearly every day. Pick out the activities you like best, and give yourself credit for the physically active daily chores you may or may not like. Use Tables 4.1 through 4.3 to see how many points you'll earn from each activity, then add them up to be sure you get at least 1,000 CME points a week, or about 150 points a day. If you are starting at a low level, give yourself some time to build up to that goal (see Table 8.1 starting on page 137). Remember that you can divide your activities into short segments, accumulating your CME points in bits and pieces toward your daily goal.

FIGURE 8.1 The No Sweat Basic Pyramid

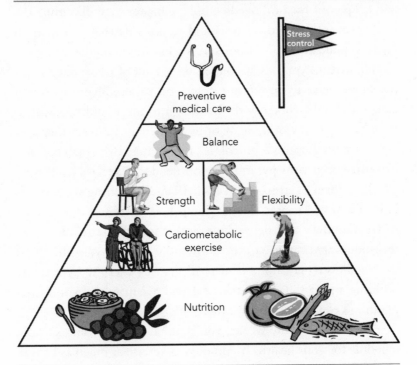

The basic pyramid moves up to add units for strength, flexibility, and balance training. Use the self-assessment tests in Chapter 3 to see how much space you should give each in your personal pyramid. Younger, more active people may not need any designated balance exercises just now, and if they keep up with strength, flexibility, and CME activities, they will probably be able to extend this exemption far into the future. Like balance, strength and flexibility decline with age—if you let them. If you start exercising in your older years, you can reverse much of the decline, but if you start while you are at the top of the curve, you can stay close to peak for many years.

Medical care is at the pinnacle of the No Sweat Pyramids. (What else would you expect from a doctor?) But in these pyramids, the top segment is the smallest. Preventive medical care is, of course, important to maintaining good health. If you work your way up the pyramid diligently, you're more likely to stay well and keep your medical needs simple. Chapter 12 will outline the basic preventive medical tests and treatments that can help all healthy adults; it's not about exercise, but it is about health.

The Great Pyramids of Cheops were built of stone, but the No Sweat Exercise Pyramids are drawn on paper. That means you can, and should, tinker with the design to meet your needs. And in our fast-paced world, many of us can benefit from another preventive strategy: stress control. It's represented by a small flag you can place atop your pyramid if you need it. Exercise itself is an excellent form of stress control; CME and stretching are particularly effective. Chapter 10 will discuss how exercise has been used to treat anxiety and depression, and it will also cite additional techniques you can use to turn down the stress in your life.

Needless to say, none of us will get our exercise by actually building a pyramid. But Tables 8.1 and 8.2 may help you fit the pyramid's elements into your daily life.

At the end of nine weeks, you will have attained an excellent schedule for your health. If you enjoy exercise as much as I think you will and if you like the results you are experiencing, you can go further. Slowly increase the weights in your strength exercises, but don't do a full set more than three times a week. Stretch a little harder or a bit more often for flexibility, but never to the point of pain. Reduce or eliminate the balance exercises when you are stable. Above all, consider increasing your CME points; 150 points a day is excellent for health, 300 a day optimal. And if you really get into it, you can go even further—not for health per se, but for fun and fitness (see the third pyramid [Figure 8.3] and Chapter 11).

If you aim for 300 CME points a day, or about 2,000 a week, give yourself another six to eight weeks to get there. Build up slowly but steadily, always listening to your body for signals that you should slow down or even back off. Alternate higher CME days with lower point totals. Break up at least some days into chunks of activity. Explore the whole range of CME activities for variety and freshness.

TABLE 8.1 A Model Exercise Program for Basic Needs

	Day 1	Day 2	Day 3	Day 4	Day 5	Day 6	Day 7
Beginner Exercisers Start Here							
Weeks 1 and 2							
CME	25 points	25 points	40 points	25 points	45 points	20 points	45 points
Strength	—	—	—	—	—	—	—
Flexibility	10–15 minutes	—	10–15 minutes	—	10–15 minutes	—	—
Balance	5 minutes	5 minutes	5 minutes	—	5 minutes	5 minutes	—
Weeks 3 and 4							
CME	35 points	45 points	35 points	60 points	35 points	60 points	35 points
Strength	5–10 minutes	—	5–10 minutes	—	—	—	—
Flexibility	—	10–15 minutes	—	10–15 minutes	—	10–15 minutes	—
Balance	5 minutes	—	5 minutes	—	5 minutes	5 minutes	5 minutes
Week 5							
CME	75 points	50 points	75 points	50 points	75 points	60 points	60 points
Strength	—	10–15 minutes	—	10–15 minutes	—	—	—
Flexibility	10–15 minutes	—	10–15 minutes	—	—	10–15 minutes	—
Balance	—	5 minutes	—	5 minutes	5 minutes	—	5 minutes

continued

TABLE 8.1 A Model Exercise Program for Basic Needs, *continued*

	Day 1	Day 2	Day 3	Day 4	Day 5	Day 6	Day 7
Intermediate Exercisers Start Here							
Week 6							
CME	75 points	75 points	100 points	75 points	100 points	75 points	100 points
Strength	—	15–20 minutes	—	15 minutes	—	—	—
Flexibility	15 minutes	—	15 minutes	—	—	15 minutes	—
Balance	—	5 minutes	—	5 minutes	5 minutes	—	5 minutes
Moderate Exercisers Start Here							
Week 7							
CME	150 points	75 points	100 points	75 points	150 points	100 points	100 points
Strength	—	15–20 minutes	—	—	—	15–20 minutes	15–20 minutes
Flexibility	10–15 minutes	—	—	10–15 minutes	—	—	10–15 minutes
Balance	—	5 minutes	5 minutes	—	5 minutes	5 minutes	15 minutes
Week 8							
CME	150 points	100 points	150 points	100 points	150 points	150 points	100 points
Strength	—	15 minutes	—	15 minutes	—	—	15 minutes
Flexibility	10–15 minutes	—	10–15 minutes	—	—	10–15 minutes	—
Balance	—	5 minutes	—	5 minutes	5 minutes	—	5 minutes
Week 9							
CME	150 points	150 points	150 points	150 points	150 points	150 points	150 points
Strength	—	15–20 minutes	—	15–20 minutes	—	15–20 minutes	—
Flexibility	10–15 minutes	—	10–15 minutes	—	15 minutes	—	15 minutes
Balance	—	5 minutes	—	5 minutes	—	5 minutes	—

TABLE 8.2 An Alternative Schedule for Flexibility, Strength, and Balance Exercises

Day	Flexibility	Strength	Balance
1	Shoulder blade scratch	Military press	As needed
	Towel stretch	Lateral raise	
2	Hip stretch	Partial squat	As needed
	William's stretch	Bent-knee sit-up	
	Cat stretch		
3	Starter's stretch	Lateral leg raise	As needed
	Groin stretch	Hip extension	
4	—	—	Full routine
5	Towel stretch	Curl	As needed
	Shoulder blade scratch	Upright row	
6	Thigh stretch	Heel raise and dip	As needed
	Hamstring stretch	Knee extension	
	Wall lean		
7	—	—	Full routine

Although variety and personal preferences are important, many of you will choose walking as your major CME activity. It's a good choice (see Chapter 4). Start out by incorporating walking into your daily activities, then switch into walking shoes and comfortable clothes as you set aside some designated time to walk for exercise, health, and recreation. Start out every walk at a slow, strolling pace to warm up, and finish off in a leisurely fashion to cool down. Add spurts of brisk walking or hills as you improve, but head for a mall or treadmill in hostile weather, and take time off if you are injured or ill (see Chapter 9). This is a general model of a basic training schedule, so tailor it to suit your needs.

You can also tinker with the flexibility and strength schedule if you prefer to spend a few minutes at it each day instead of setting aside a block of time, however modest, on only certain days of the week. Table 8.2 shows an alternative model of strength and stretching scheduling. It uses flexibility to warm up for lifting, and it rotates you through different muscle groups to allow you to recover properly. Work in parts of your balance routine as you see fit. Remember to do the "anywhere, anytime" exercises whenever you can (according to need).

Be creative as you design your own schedule, and don't hesitate to experiment with new variations on the basic theme. Remember that stretching and leisurely walking are excellent for the warm-up and cooldown periods that should precede and follow every major exercise session. They are also good ways to keep moderate to strenuous daily activities and physically demanding chores safe and injury free. Even without stretching or strolling, most tasks have some built-in restraints; for example, you have to get out the tools before you garden and put them away afterward.

Try to exercise every day or nearly every day. Illness and injury are important exceptions to the rule (see Chapter 9), but even then, some gentle stretching or other substitute activities may be appropriate. Fortunately, sustained medical exceptions are uncommon. Unfortunately, though, the hustle and bustle of daily life often get in the way of daily exercise, and all too often a few days off becomes the slippery slope back to sloth. Don't let that happen. At the end of this chapter, I'll give you some tips for overcoming obstacles to regular exercise.

TABLE 8.3 Sample Exercise Log

Week of _____

Weight (at start of week) _____

Waist size (record once a month) _____

	CME	Strength	Flexibility	Balance	Comments
Monday					
Tuesday					
Wednesday					
Thursday					
Friday					
Saturday					
Sunday					

One good way to stay on track is to keep track of your progress. Repeat your self-assessment tests from Chapter 3 to document your improvement; nothing motivates like success. If weight loss is a goal, keep track of your weight and waist size. Keep an exercise log to chart these developments and to be sure you are sticking to your plan. Table 8.3 shows a sample log. In the "CME" column, record your CME activities, total points, and approximate intensity level on the Borg scale (see Table 4.4). In the "Strength" column, record the exercises you performed, the weights used, and the number of sets and reps. In the "Flexibility" and "Balance" columns, list the exercises you did each day. Finally, in the "Comments" column, record any positive or negative experiences or sensations and any lessons you learned or new goals you established. Make copies of the log that you can fill in each week, at least during the early months of your exercise program.

The No Sweat Pyramid for Weight Loss

At least two out of three American adults need to lose weight. For years, being overweight was considered a cosmetic issue, but it's now clear that it is also a very serious medical problem. In 2004 Medicare recognized obesity as a disease for the first time in history. That should allow coverage for medically sound weight-loss programs. It's good news, but it overlooks the fact that two essential elements of successful weight loss are free. One is caloric restriction. The other is exercise.

The math is simple but unyielding: to lose weight, you must burn up more calories than you take in. The greater the gap, the faster the weight loss. It's hard for many people to accept the formula, which is why diet schemes rake in millions upon millions of dollars each year. Unfortunately, the steady stream of miraculous new plans is testimony to the fact that none of the old ones have lived up to their hype.

Have a look at the weight-loss pyramid (see Figure 8.2). The nutrition block is not any smaller. Although you'll need to con-

FIGURE 8.2 The No Sweat Pyramid for Weight Loss

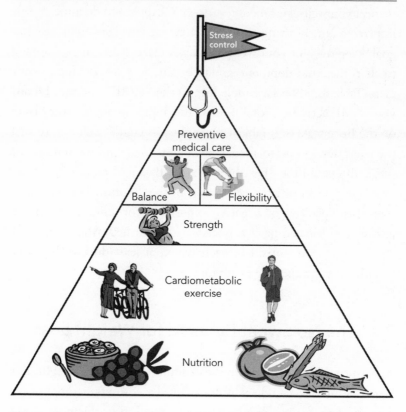

sume fewer calories, you'll need to pay at least as much attention to planning a balanced, healthful diet; Chapter 12 reviews the principles of good nutrition. For weight loss (and also for good health in the lucky third of us who are lean), reduce your consumption of calorie-dense foods, such as simple sugars and sweets and fats. For your heart's sake, saturated fat from animal sources and trans fat from stick margarine, fried foods, and many processed foods should be the first to go. Substitute filling, low-calorie, nutrient-rich foods, such as fruits, vegetables, and whole grains.

The big change in the weight–loss pyramid is the increase in the CME block. CME burns calories. You can lose weight with

150 points a day, but you'll lose faster with 300 points or more—and you'll also gain a bit of wiggle room in your diet. That's why the Institute of Medicine recommends an hour of moderate exercise a day for weight loss, while the surgeon general recommends thirty minutes a day for general health.

The weight-loss pyramid also has an expanded strength component. Muscle cells burn calories faster than fat cells; building up your muscles with resistance exercise will help you shrink your fat cells. Contrary to some claims, though, no form of treatment can turn fat into muscle.

The final change in the weight-loss pyramid is that the stress control flag is flying atop the pyramid. It's hoisted up because the behavioral changes required for successful weight loss are stressful and difficult. Although caloric restriction and exercise sound obvious, they may often require counseling and supervision to succeed, which is why insurance coverage is important.

The Great Pyramids of ancient Egypt were built by slaves. But you don't have to enslave yourself or spend big bucks to lose weight. On the contrary, moderate exercise and a healthful diet are enjoyable and fulfilling. The No Sweat Exercise Pyramid for Weight Loss can set you free.

 ## The No Sweat Pyramid for Sports and Competition

Nutrition, as always the foundation for health, is in its familiar place on the third No Sweat Pyramid (see Figure 8.3). But the exercise blocks are different. Moderate-intensity CME activities are still there—after all, all able-bodied people should walk the stairs. But there is a second CME block, for high-intensity CME and aerobic exercises. Both moderate and aerobic-intensity exercises are excellent for health, but aerobics gets the nod for promoting the fitness and endurance required for sports and competition. The more demanding the sport, the more training

FIGURE 8.3 The No Sweat Pyramid for Sports

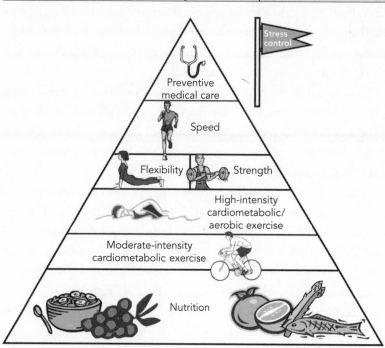

you'll need. Chapter 11 will outline the medical aspects of some common sports.

Flexibility and strength training are of obvious importance to athletes. Muscle power is a requirement for nearly all sports, but some require more strength (sprinting and rowing, for example) while others require more endurance (distance running and Nordic skiing, for example). And since muscles get tighter and shorter as they get stronger, flexibility training will help most athletes stretch their performances and shrink their injuries.

Balance training is gone. Most sporting activities provide plenty of that, and most athletes have excellent balance and coordination. Remember, for example, that elderly golfers have the same good (and youthful!) sense of balance as age–matched tai chi practitioners (see Chapters 4 and 7).

The sports pyramid has another new block: speed training. It's not necessary for moderate-intensity skill sports, such as golf, but it is a great asset for sports that require bursts of speed. Running, singles racquet sports, and competitive swimming and biking are examples.

Speed training is hard work, very hard. It means pushing yourself nearly to the top of the Borg scale (see Table 4.4) so your heart is pounding, your lungs are gasping, and your muscles are aching. Then, mercifully, you back off—but for serious competitive training, you do it all over again, and then again and again.

Athletes have to get into good shape before they even begin speed drills. They must be diligent about stretching, warming up, and cooling down. And speed drills must be carefully planned and monitored. They should never push you to the point of exhaustion and collapse, and they must always be interspersed with periods of sharply reduced exercise intensity. This "on again, off again" method is called interval training. It's the same approach that will help you build from strolling to brisk walking and then, if you choose, to jogging (see Chapter 11).

Speed drills are very helpful, even mandatory, for certain competitive athletes. But they pose a substantial risk for injury without adding health benefit.

It's interesting to know what sleek young jocks do to prepare for their big events. Still, speed training is not recommended for ordinary mortals, much less folks who are faint of heart. But there is a final No Sweat Pyramid, for people with medical issues.

The No Sweat Pyramid for People with Medical Problems, Low Fitness, or Advancing Age

The final pyramid is for people with special needs (see Figure 8.4). As such, it requires the most individual modification to meet these needs.

FIGURE 8.4 The No Sweat Pyramid for Medical Problems

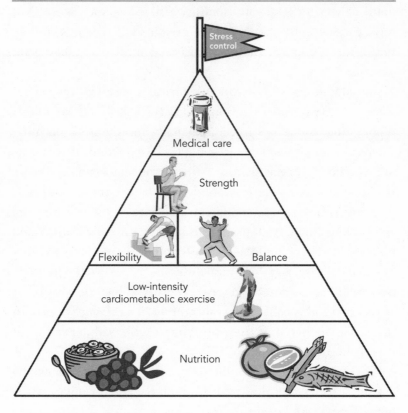

Many people with chronic illnesses have special dietary requirements. As a result, the nutrition block may well benefit from professional supervision by a physician, a nurse, or (best of all) a registered dietitian.

Nearly everyone can benefit from CME activities. But folks who are elderly or ill need to go easy and to exercise special care. The same is true for stretching and, especially, for strength training. Muscle weakness is all but universal in people who are elderly or ill. They stand to gain the most from strength exercise, not because it will make them into athletes (it won't) but because it can enable essential daily activities that might otherwise be difficult or impossible. In fact, exercise is now standard therapy for many patients who were formerly advised to rest; congestive heart failure and peripheral artery disease are examples (see Chapter 10).

All forms of exercise require special evaluation, precautions, and supervision for people who are challenged by illness or age. That's why the fourth No Sweat Pyramid has a greatly expanded medical care component. And since the body and mind are inseparable parts of the human organism, the stress control flag is attached to this pyramid. If nothing else, it's a reminder that special mental effort is required to ensure compliance with the medical treatments, dietary regulations, and exercise regimens on the pyramid.

Although nearly everyone can and should exercise, people with medical problems may well have legitimate reasons to claim exemption from the rule. Unfortunately, many healthy people raise similar objections. We are all human, and it can be hard to adopt an active lifestyle in a society that has changed exercise from a necessity to a luxury. But with a little thought, you can jump over most barriers to exercise.

Overcoming Obstacles

In thirty-five years of medical practice, I've heard them all. All start the same way: "I can't exercise because . . ." And they all end with a statement that seems perfectly reasonable. Indeed, many are legitimate problems, and a few are nearly insoluble. But most barriers to exercise can be overcome with a little thought, a little effort, and a good dose of motivation.

Here are some of the excuses I've heard from my patients and some tips for dealing with them:

"I don't have the time."
It's the most common excuse, and it's a real problem for many of us. Life is busy, and you'll never *find* the time to exercise. But you

can *make* the time. The No Sweat plan for moderate exercise is a big help. You can accumulate your CME points in small chunks that you can squeeze into a busy day. You can climb stairs, walk from point A to point B, and find many other physically active ways to accomplish your daily tasks while also earning CME points. You can divide up your stretching and strength training so it takes just a few minutes each day. And you can also make time for designated exercise. Give up some sleep; exercise will make you more energetic, and it will help you sleep better, so you won't miss the shut-eye. Walk with your friends instead of meeting them for coffee or lunch. Spend some of your lunch hour walking; remember that you can earn your CME points without changing into athletic togs or breaking into a sweat. Do more on weekends, holidays, and vacations, but do something important for your body and your health nearly every day. Be creative and crafty: you can make exercise happen. For perspective, remember that thirty to forty-five minutes represents just 2 to 3 percent of your day. And in the final analysis, it's a remarkable bargain, since you'll gain about an hour of life expectancy for every thirty minutes of regular exercise. In a sense, exercise will allow you to turn energy into time. You don't have to be an Einstein to see that exercise matters—not relatively, but absolutely.

"I don't like to exercise."

Give it time. The first steps are hardest, but if you stick with exercise for three months, it's likely you'll come to enjoy it. Remember that you don't have to walk, much less run. Look over the huge range of daily activities and recreational pursuits that will earn CME points, and pick the ones you like the best. Everybody likes some form of physical activity—and the more you do, the more you'll like.

"It's boring."

This is an easy one. See "I don't like to exercise" to understand that many interesting options are available. And there's much more you can do to stay amused.

- If you like company, exercise with a friend. Moderate exercise will allow you to chat to your heart's content.
- If you like to watch TV or movies, put a treadmill or stationary bike in front of your TV and DVD player.
- If you like to read, try newspapers, magazines, or books while pedaling a stationary bike; if you find it hard to focus, buy large-print publications.
- If you like music, hook yourself up to headphones and a portable player. You can also "read" with your ears: rent, buy, or borrow a book on tape and turn it on while you exercise. For extra motivation, listen to the book only during exercise; there's nothing like an engrossing tale to make the time fly.
- If you like pets, walk a dog.
- And if all else fails, just remind yourself that convalescing from a heart attack or colon cancer surgery is significantly more boring than the exercise that will help keep you healthy.

"I'm too fat."

It's true that exercise is harder for people who are obese than for the svelte set. But it's also more important, and it's an essential requirement for sustained weight loss. Pick a low-impact activity, start out easy, and build up gradually. One caveat: although swimming has many advantages for people who are overweight, it does not promote weight loss as well as land exercise does.

"I'm embarrassed."

Get an appropriate machine and exercise in the privacy of your home (see Chapter 11). Chances are you'll gain the confidence to go public as you get in shape. To speed that up, take a look at the runners in a local road race. They come in all shapes and sizes, and some of the most awkward looking are mighty speedy. Think of the clumsiest exercisers that you've seen; if they can exercise, so can you. If you don't know any athletes who qualify, feel free to think of me!

"I don't have the money."

Another easy one. Physically active daily tasks are free—in fact, you'll actually save money by washing the car or mowing the lawn yourself. You can walk in good street shoes, and when you move on, you can find walking shoes for a low price at outlet stores. Look for off-brands and factory seconds, but be sure they fit well and give you plenty of support and cushioning. Use towels instead of a mat for floor exercises, and buy inexpensive iron weights or elastic bands for strength training. If you need instruction or prefer group activities, check out your local high school, Y, or community center.

"I have bad feet [or legs]."

Use your arms. Remember the example of Scott Simons (see Chapter 4), who has drummed his way to fitness. True, he likes to practice his musical avocation, but he also has orthopedic problems that make lower-body exercise difficult. Many health clubs have arm ergometers for upper-body exercise. Try aquatic exercise or low-impact land activities. Best of all, see a podiatrist, an orthopedist, or a physical therapist to get help with your feet and legs.

"I have to watch my kids."

If they are infants or toddlers, exercise at home while they nap; pedal a stationary bike while they play or read. Push them in a stroller while you walk. Join a gym that has day care. And when they're old enough, get them involved in a game of tag or hopscotch, or build an obstacle course and race them through it. Plan family activities that will get you all moving, such as biking or swimming.

"I don't know how."

Sure you do. Almost any physical activity will earn at least a few CME points. Even if you've never mounted a bike or held a racquet, you can walk, climb stairs, and do simple strength and flexibility exercises. You can also learn new skills from books, videos, and lessons.

"Something always comes up at work, and I get home too late to exercise before dinner."

Another common problem. Exercising after dinner is not a good solution, since a full stomach will put extra stress on your heart and circulation (see Chapter 9). Try to get in a walk or a trip to a nearby gym at lunchtime. Many enlightened companies provide exercise facilities on site; see if you can get your employer to consider adding one—it's good for morale, and it will cut down on health care expenses and absenteeism. Unfortunately, corporate policy is not in your control. Fortunately, however, you can control your own schedule. For many of us that means getting up early enough to exercise before work. You have most control over your schedule before the demands of work and family kick in. And you won't miss the sleep nearly as much as you think. Be particularly careful to warm up thoroughly before early morning exercise, since adrenaline levels, blood pressure, and cardiac risk all peak in the wee hours.

"I used to exercise and I felt better. But for some reason I stopped."

Start over, and this time make exercise a part of every day. Keep an exercise log to be sure you don't fall off your bike again.

"I get plenty of exercise already."

Perhaps. Check the tables in Chapter 3 to see if you're right. If so, you have my congratulations. But if it's wishful thinking, take steps to make your perception a reality.

"My neighborhood is not safe."

Exercise in your home or travel to a better location. Walk at the mall, join a gym, or walk before or after work or at lunchtime. If you can make time, you can make a place, too.

"I'm afraid I'll get arthritis."

You won't—or, at least, you won't get it from exercise. Moderate exercise in the No Sweat venue is easy on the joints. In fact, even high-impact sports like running are safe for joints. Most studies find no link between running and arthritis, and some actually report that long-distance running is associated with a substantial reduction in the risk of musculoskeletal problems and disability.

"I have heart disease [or diabetes, arthritis, or other medical problems]."

You will need medical clearance before you exercise, and you will probably need an individual exercise prescription. Cardiac patients, in particular, should have stress tests and, if possible, supervision in a cardiac rehab program as they learn to monitor themselves. All in all, though, some form of exercise is suitable for most patients, and exercise is actually an effective treatment for many conditions (see Chapter 10).

"I'm too old."

Not likely. Old age is not an illness, but it does require modifications as noted earlier and on the fourth No Sweat Pyramid (see Figure 8.4). It's never too late to start; before you use the calendar to cop out of exercise, remember that frail institutionalized octogenarians benefit from strength training. Exercise will actually make your body "younger" at any age.

"I'm too tired; I don't have enough energy."

It may be the worst excuse of all. Inactivity produces fatigue and lethargy. Exercise promotes vigor and energy. Try it and see. You may have to drag yourself out at first, but if you stick with it, in time you'll have to hold yourself back.

"It hurts."

Most likely you're doing too much too soon or too little stretching and warming up. Chapter 9 will explain how to prevent, recognize, and correct common exercise-induced aches and pains. If you can't do it yourself, get professional help. Exercise should not be painful, and No Sweat exercise shouldn't even feel hard.

"I get winded."

That's exactly why you need to exercise. And always remember to warm up, start out gradually, and pace yourself properly. Healthy people should never huff and puff during moderate exercise.

"Jim Fixx."

Even if you don't remember the tragic case of the jogging guru who died while running in 1984, you've probably heard of some-one famous who has had a heart attack while exercising. It's rare, but it gets plenty of press. In fact, regular exercise will sharply reduce your risk of heart attack and sudden cardiac death (see Chapter 1). Moderate exercise is even safer than intense activity, but it's still serious business. That's why you should pay heed to the precautions discussed in the next chapter.

People have lots of reasons for not exercising—but doctors have many more reasons why exercise should be woven into the fabric of daily life. View exercise as an opportunity, not a chore. Be grateful for all the options and opportunities at your disposal. Above all, consider your priorities. If good health is a high prior-ity for you, exercise will become one, too. Make it happen.

CHAPTER 9

Pitfalls and Precautions

Keeping Exercise Safe

The greatest hazard of exercise is not doing it. Far more people are harmed by the lack of exercise than by its excess. That includes about 250,000 people who die prematurely in the United States each year, to say nothing of the hundreds of thousands who suffer because of heart attacks, hypertension, strokes, cancers, fractures, diabetes, and obesity that could be prevented by moderate exercise. But while the benefits of exercise far outweigh the risks, there are risks. The good news is that moderate-intensity exercise is intrinsically safer than high-intensity and even aerobic-intensity exercise. And a few simple precautions will go a long way toward keeping exercise safe and enjoyable.

Pitfalls

The most frequent complications of exercise are injuries to the tissues that power physical activity (see the following sections). But the heart muscle is also put to work during exercise. Cardiovascular complications are uncommon, and they are particularly unlikely to develop during moderate-intensity activity. Still, you should know how to protect your heart during exercise.

Cardiac Complications of Exercise

First the bad news: exercise can precipitate heart attacks and sudden cardiac death. Now the good news: it's rare. But in man-bites-dog fashion, exercise-induced deaths get all the publicity. People who die during sleep make the obituary page, but people who die playing ball make the front page.

Exercise-induced cardiac deaths fall into two distinct groups.

In young athletes, the cause is usually an inborn abnormality of the coronary arteries, an abnormal thickening of the heart muscle (*hypertrophic cardiomyopathy*), inflammation of the heart muscle (*myocarditis*), or a noncardiac problem, such as drug abuse. Young athletes should protect themselves by following simple precautions. A competent physical examination should precede competition. Athletes with heart murmurs should be considered for further testing, including EKGs and echocardiograms; so, too, should athletes whose families sport histories of premature or exercise-induced deaths. Above all, athletes must learn to listen to their bodies, promptly reporting dizziness, faintness, chest pain, palpitations, undue breathlessness, or other unusual occurrences during exercise. And, like all of us, young athletes should avoid strenuous exercise when they have the flu or other viral infections.

In middle-aged and older people, sudden death during exercise usually results from coronary artery disease and heart attacks. Jogging guru Jim Fixx is a tragic example. Although he was a highly conditioned athlete, he died at age fifty-two from a heart attack that occurred while he was running in Vermont. But Fixx had risk factors, including former tobacco abuse and a strong family history of early cardiac death. He had been sedentary and overweight for most of his life. As a person who shares many of these traits, I share your worries about exercise-induced heart problems. But I won't share another factor common to Fixx and most other middle-aged people who die during exercise: they experience chest discomfort during exertion but fail to get medical attention. The best way to protect your heart during exercise is to prevent atherosclerosis before it occurs; the second best way is to listen to your body.

Exercise-induced cardiac death is rare. Dr. Kenneth Cooper's Aerobics Center has not recorded any in more than 375,000 hours of exercise, including 1.2 million miles of walking and jogging. Other studies report that cardiac arrests occur about once for every 565,000 person-hours of vigorous exercise by individuals who did not have known heart disease.

How can you protect yourself from becoming the exception to the rule that exercise is good for your heart? As discussed a little later, getting medical checkups and remaining alert for symptoms are essential. But although it may seem paradoxical, regular exercise is also protective. Researchers in Seattle found that sedentary people who engage in strenuous exercise without first working themselves into shape are fifty-six times more likely to die during an hour of exercise than during a sedentary hour. People who exercise regularly also experience an increased risk during peak exertion, but that risk is less than one-tenth as high and—most important—their overall risk of sudden cardiac death is 60 percent lower than the risk of sedentary people. And in a more recent report, the Harvard-sponsored Physicians' Health Study agreed. The risk of sudden death was almost seventeen times higher during and up to thirty minutes after a bout of vigorous exercise than during a similar time span with little or no exercise. As in the Seattle study, though, regular exercise substantially reduced the cardiac hazards of intense exertion. Best of all, the risks were extremely low, amounting to just one sudden death per 1.51 million bouts of exercise, even when out-of-shape men were included in the analysis.

Exercise can also trigger nonfatal heart attacks; most are caused by the rupture of an atherosclerotic plaque in a coronary artery (see Chapter 1). A European study of almost twelve hundred heart attack patients found that about 7 percent had been engaged in moderate-to-intense physical exertion at the time of their attacks. But most of these problems developed in people who exercised fewer than four times a week; in fact, regular exercisers were about 85 percent less likely to have heart attacks during exercise than were "weekend warriors."

In addition to sudden cardiac death and heart attacks, exercise can precipitate *arrhythmias*, disorders of the heart's pumping rhythm. By now you should be able to anticipate the rest of the story: these problems are uncommon with vigorous exercise and less frequent still with moderate exercise, and they occur much less often in people who exercise regularly than in those who don't.

Doctors know that heart attacks and sudden cardiac deaths are more common in the early morning hours. Should you avoid exercise in the morning? It's a good question, with a good answer: exercise is equally safe at any time of the day, if it's done right. The best evidence comes from Dr. Paul Murray's 1993 study of nearly three hundred cardiac rehabilitation patients who were monitored during a total of more than 252,000 hours of exercise. About half exercised regularly at 7:30 A.M., the rest at 3:00 P.M. Even in these patients with heart disease, exercise was equally safe in the morning and afternoon. It's reassuring news, particularly since morning exercise is most convenient for many people. But if you work out in the morning, remember to warm up diligently and to delay breakfast until afterward.

Cardiac complications of exercise are uncommon, and most occur during vigorous exertion (such as running) rather than during moderate exercise (such as walking). According to the Myocardial Infarct (heart attack) Onset Study, vigorous exercise is about five times more likely to trigger an attack than moderate exercise. Still, everyone who exercises should protect themselves by getting medical checkups and by knowing how to recognize and respond to warning symptoms.

Healthy adults who have been getting regular medical care (see Chapter 12) don't need a special evaluation before starting moderate exercise. Your regular checkups should include an evaluation of your family history and your health habits as well as a review of any symptoms you may have. Your physicals should include a check of your blood pressure, your heart and lungs, your pulses, and your joints. Useful lab tests include a complete blood count, cholesterol profile, and blood sugar level. Periodic electrocardiograms are reasonable after age forty, particularly if you haven't had one within five years. If you've passed these tests, you can begin to exercise without additional evaluations. But if you have a moderate or high cardiac risk profile (see Chapter 3), you should check with your physician first.

Should you have a stress test prior to exercise? The theory is appealing: if you exercise in a hospital lab with an EKG hooked up and medical personnel in attendance, perhaps you'll be able to detect heart problems so that they won't occur when you're out jogging on the roads. Appealing or not, stress tests have not proved beneficial for routine preexercise screening. The best evidence comes from a 1991 study of 3,617 asymptomatic men aged thirty-five to fifty-nine who were at high risk for heart disease because of high cholesterol levels. Even in these high-risk people, annual stress tests were not able to predict exercise-induced cardiac problems before they occurred. The good news, though, is that such problems were rare, occurring in only 2 percent of subjects during seven years of exercise. Still, if you have any cardiac symptoms, you should have a stress test before you begin exercising. The same is true for everyone with suspected or diagnosed heart disease or atherosclerosis.

What symptoms should alert you to the possibility that exercise is overstressing your heart? They are the same symptoms of angina or heart attacks that we should always heed, but they're a little harder to notice during exercise because of the "background noise" of heavy breathing that's a normal part of vigorous exercise. Still, "listen" for chest pressure, tightness, or pain. Be alert for disproportionate shortness of breath, fatigue, or sweating. Take note of dizziness, light-headedness, faintness, or an irregular or unduly rapid heartbeat. Even "indigestion" warrants your attention if it comes on during exercise. Most often, these symptoms are not actually signs of heart trouble, but you should not take a chance. Instead, stop exercising at once and report the symptoms to your doctor. Remember what we teach medical students: chest pain is the most common symptom of heart trouble, denial the second most common.

One last observation about exercise and cardiac risk: a small study from Maryland reported that middle-aged men who stop exercising can develop evidence of heart disease during their layoffs. It's another illustration of the general rule that the lack of exercise is a hazard to your health.

Exercise-Induced Lung Problems

In most people, exercise eases the flow of air into the lungs by widening the bronchial tubes. But in about 10 percent of us, the reverse occurs: exercise produces narrowing of bronchial tubes, a condition called *exercise-induced asthma* (EIA).

EIA can be mild or severe. Symptoms include various combinations of coughing, wheezing, shortness of breath, and chest discomfort. In some people, the only symptom is reduced endurance or impaired athletic performance.

Attacks of EIA occur most often during intense exertion in cold, dry air. Cutting back to moderate exercise and heading to the gym on frosty winter days will control many problems. Because of the warmth and humidity, swimming is a particularly good sport for people with EIA or, for that matter, ordinary asthma. But if these simple precautions don't do the trick, prescription medications can almost always control the problem.

Exercising at New Heights

Oxygen levels are highest at sea level, but they fall steadily at increasing altitudes. Most people won't notice any effect until about five thousand feet; even when you're one mile above sea level, breathing is comfortable at rest, but it becomes labored with exertion. And the higher you go, the harder your lungs have to work to take in the oxygen you need. By eight thousand feet, things get dicey. That's the altitude of many western U.S. ski resorts and of some of the most beautiful spots in our national parks. Most sightseers will feel fine at eight thousand feet, but the stress of skiing or hiking can trigger problems, especially in older people. A few simple precautions can prevent nearly all problems, at least at moderate altitude:

- Be sure you are in good shape before you travel.
- Ascend gradually. You can fly to Denver or Mexico City in one hop, but if you are going higher, a few days of acclimation will be worth your time. Above eight thousand feet, don't go up more than a thousand feet a day.
- Limit your exercise during your first days at altitude, and take it easy throughout your trip if you have medical problems or if you feel at all unwell.
- Drink plenty of fluids.
- Avoid or minimize your alcohol consumption, particularly for the first forty-eight hours at altitude. Avoid sedatives.
- Be alert for symptoms such as breathlessness, chest discomfort, headache, nausea, fatigue, and confusion. Don't ignore symptoms; instead, get down to lower elevation and get help.
- Ask your doctor about *acetazolamide* (Diamox), a prescription drug that can facilitate acclimatization and lessen the risk of mountain sickness; it is a mild diuretic that stimulates

breathing by causing the kidneys to secrete bicarbonate and sodium in the urine.

▪ Above all, exercise restraint. Although I've urged you to exercise at moderate intensity nearly every day, people in high places should take a few days off and then resume exercise at modest levels they would consider easy back home.

Intestinal Complaints

Scientists believe that increased intestinal motility helps explain why exercise reduces the risk of colon cancer (see Chapter 1). That's a good thing. Unfortunately, it can also be a nuisance, causing belching, heartburn, nausea, or diarrhea (the "runner's trots"). Most of these problems can be managed simply by exercising on an empty stomach. Antacids can also help; if diarrhea is a concern, select an antacid that has calcium carbonate (Tums, for example) rather than magnesium hydroxide (Maalox, for example).

Reproductive and Sexual Concerns

Exercise helps protect women from breast cancer (see Chapter 1), and it may reduce their risk of cancer of the uterus and of *endometriosis*, a benign but painful reproductive condition. All it takes to get these benefits is moderate exercise. On the other hand, intense exercise can delay the onset of menstruation in girls, and it can cause mature women to stop having their periods. But these problems result from the combination of intense exercise and substantial weight loss. Treatment is simple but highly effective: reduced exercise and increased body fat. Moderate exercise is exempt from these complications.

Exercise rarely causes sexual dysfunction in males, with one important exception: biking. The problem here is not exercise itself, but the bicycle seat, which can put pressure on the nerves and arteries responsible for erections. If the bicycle seat is the problem, it can also be the solution for men who ride regularly. Pick a wide seat, ideally with plenty of padding. Special gel-filled and shock-absorbing seats are even available. Don't tilt your seat to the forward position, which increases pressure on your bottom. Be sure the seat height is correct, so that your legs are not completely straightened at the bottom of your pedal stroke. And for extra protection, consider wearing padded biking pants.

In some circumstances, exercise can affect sexuality. But sex is, among other things, a form of exercise. Is this rather special type of exertion safe? Disappointingly, perhaps, people seem to spend more energy thinking and talking about sex than on the act itself. During sexual intercourse, the heart rate rarely gets as high as 130 beats a minute, and the systolic blood pressure (the higher number, recorded when the heart is pumping blood) nearly always stays under 170. All in all, average sexual activity ranks as mild to moderate in exercise intensity, about the same as doing the fox-trot or raking leaves. Sex burns about five calories a minute; that's four more than a person uses watching TV, but it's about the same as walking the course to play golf. If you can walk up two or three flights of stairs without difficulty, you should be in shape for sex.

Unless you are unusually active, sex won't help you bring up your CME score (see Table 4.3). But unless you have unstable heart disease, you don't need any special precautions for this modest form of exercise.

Exercising in the Heat

Sex may be a hot topic, but hot weather is a bigger hazard, at least as far as exercise is concerned. Even on a crisp November day, your body has to work at staying cool. That's because your body generates heat as a by-product of all its metabolic processes. And exercise ups the ante: at peak exertion, you can produce up to twenty times more heat than at rest.

Heat-related illnesses result from an imbalance between human behavior and Mother Nature. Nature contributes high air temperatures, high humidity, the radiant energy of sunlight, and still air. You can't do much to change nature, but you can control the human elements that contribute to heat illnesses; unwise exercise, undue exposure to sun and heat, inappropriate clothing, and dehydration head the list. Three types of problems can result:

- **Heat cramps.** Most of us experience muscle cramps from time to time. It's OK to dismiss the occasional cramp as a simple charley horse, but if you get recurrent cramps in hot weather, you could be heading for trouble. The remedy: slow down, tank up with cool water, stretch out and gently massage the tight muscle, and get out of the heat.

- **Heat exhaustion.** Heat cramps are painful but not threatening; that's because body temperature is normal even though muscles are in spasm. But in heat exhaustion, body temperature is high, often above 103°F. Other symptoms include weakness, lethargy, loss of concentration, headache, and nausea; muscle cramps may also occur.

  Heat exhaustion impairs mental clarity and judgment, so you may not recognize the problem as it develops. Be alert for early symptoms and take corrective action as soon as they appear. Be watchful, too, of signs of heat exhaustion in others; confusion, profuse sweating, and flushed, clammy skin are among the tip-offs. Move victims to a cool place as soon as possible; remove their clothing and fan them en route. You should apply ice packs if they're available, cool fluids if not. Cool fluids on the skin will lower body temperature, but it's even more important to get them down the hatch. Don't force someone who is weak and confused to drink too much too fast, but keep at it until hydration is restored.

- **External heat stroke.** It's the illness that kills each and every summer, even with treatment. The typical victim is a man who exercises vigorously in the first few days of a hot spell; many are young, but most are out of shape. Marine recruits and weekend warriors exemplify men at risk; heavy clothing, exposure to direct sunlight, and dehydration often add fuel to the fire.

Heat stroke is a medical emergency. It starts out looking like heat exhaustion, but its symptoms are more severe and they progress more quickly, as lethargy, weakness, and confusion evolve into delirium, stupor, coma, and seizures. Body temperature rises drastically, often exceeding 105 or 106°F. Even with so much excess body heat, the victim's skin may be pale and inappropriately dry due to a failure of normal sweating.

Heat stroke is a killer because it damages the heart, liver, kidneys, brain, and blood clotting system. Survival depends on prompt transfer to an emergency ward for aggressive treatment. Expert metabolic and cardiovascular care is mandatory, but even in this era of high-tech medicine, the best way to lower a heat stroke patient's temperature is to immerse him in a bath of ice water or to spray him with cold water and turn on a strong fan.

An ounce of prevention will go a long way, but for heat-related illnesses, a quart is even better. That's because hydration is essential, and it takes a lot of liquid to preserve your body's circulation and replace the fluid lost in sweat. Even if you're sedentary, you may need ten to twelve cups of water a day in hot weather; if you exercise, you'll need much more. Cool liquids are best; despite the popularity of sports drinks, nothing beats water.

Hydration is necessary, but it's not sufficient on its own to stave off summertime heat. Here are a few important tips:

- Don't exercise when it's hot or humid. If it's humid and above 75 to 80°F, jump in a pool or work out in an air-conditioned gym. If you exercise outdoors, do it in the early morning or evening. Slow down; walk instead of jogging or use a cart instead of walking the golf course. Take breaks and quit early.
- Stay out of the sun and avoid the midday heat as much as possible. Wear brief, loose-fitting, light-colored garments.

- Get away from the heat. An air-conditioned room is best, but even a fan will help. If you can't cool your own home, take refuge with a friend or relative.
- Above all, listen to your body. Muscle cramps, fatigue, weakness, impaired concentration, confusion, light-headedness, nausea, labored breathing, chest discomfort, and a rapid or erratic pulse can all be signs of trouble. Heed your body's warning signals; if you feel ill—even a little ill—get to a cool place, drink plenty of cool water, and be sure help is available if you don't improve promptly.

Exercising in the Cold

Since physical activities generate heat, cold weather should be great for exercise. That's true—but only up to a point. Shakespeare warned of "barren winter, with his wrathful nipping cold." It's a valuable caution even after four hundred years, but many of us do our best to remain active outdoors even in the depths of winter.

Most cold weather injuries are not caused by low temperatures alone. Moisture is a particularly hazardous condition; it can come in the form of rain, snow, or accidental immersion, or it can occur when sweat accumulates on cold, vulnerable skin. Another important risk factor is age; very young children are especially prone to cold weather injuries, as are older adults. Injuries or illnesses that prevent a person from staying active also increase risk. Alcohol or drugs that impair judgment are additional things that can turn insult into injury. Disorders of the heart and circulation that restrict the delivery of warm blood to cool tissues and nerve diseases that blunt the early warning signals of tingling and pain also increase risk. And in many cases, the culprits are poor planning and bad judgment; appropriate clothing and good old common sense could prevent the four most common problems:

- **Frostnip.** The mildest type of freezing injury, frostnip usually occurs in cool tissues, often striking the fingers, toes, ears, or nose. The damaged tissues feel cold and painful, but they never become completely numb. Appropriate warming leads to full recovery.

- **Superficial frostbite.** You may be glad when the pain of frostnip goes away, but if you're still out in the cold, the loss of pain should be alarming, not reassuring. That's because frozen nerves stop sending the warning signals of pain, and in frostbite the skin is frozen along with its nerves and fatty supporting tissues.
- **Deep frostbite.** This occurs when the cold exposure is so severe that freezing injury extends all the way down to muscles and tendons. The skin remains pale and numb even during rewarming. Deep frostbite can produce permanent damage with loss of function and disfigurement.
- **Hypothermia.** This occurs in stages. When body temperature begins to dip below normal, the victim paces around and shivers to warm up. But if injury, exhaustion, or intoxication prevent muscular activity, or if the cold exposure is intense and prolonged, body temperature continues to plummet. At temperatures below 95°F, people become apathetic and lethargic and often slur their speech. Without treatment, hypothermia patients lapse into comas and die.

The treatment of cold weather injuries begins with rewarming. In the case of skin injuries, a warm whirlpool or tub works best; the water should be 100 to 110°F. It takes twenty to sixty minutes for tissues to warm and thaw, but rewarming can produce intense pain. The injured tissues are fragile and must not be over-heated or traumatized. Frostnip and mild frostbite can be treated at home, but deep frostbite requires expert medical attention that may include plastic surgery.

Hypothermia must be treated promptly and aggressively. Cold or wet clothing should be removed and replaced by warm blankets. If the victim is alert, he or she should be given warm fluids.

Hot water bottles or other forms of active warming may be required in severe cases. And hypothermia patients should always be evacuated to a hospital for monitoring and treatment.

As with all exercise-related problems, the best treatment for cold weather injuries is prevention. The basics are simple: stay warm and dry. That means staying indoors when the windchill is dangerously low or when it's wet. In less extreme conditions, wear layers of clothing; fabrics that wick away moisture, such as wool or polypropylene, are best. Take particular care to cover your face and ears and to protect your hands and feet. Above all, use common sense.

Snow Shoveling

It sounds like a particularly good form of winter exercise. The overall intensity is moderate, similar to brisk walking or active doubles tennis. It gets you outdoors in fresh air, but it keeps you close to the warmth and safety of home. And it accomplishes an important chore that will help prevent accidents and injury.

Although snow shoveling may sound like a good idea, it's anything but. In fact, it's the one form of exercise I discourage, particularly for people at risk. Here's why:

- It involves cold exposure, a cardiac stress that narrows arteries and raises blood pressure.
- It uses arm and back muscles that are not well conditioned, further pumping up blood pressure.
- The work of shoveling snow comes in episodic, intense bursts, and it's isometric exercise, which raises blood pressure and most taxes the heart.
- People who shovel are often out of shape. Like weekend warriors, seasonal shovelers are at much higher risk than people who exercise regularly the year round.
- Most people don't warm up before they shovel or cool down afterward.
- It brings out the machismo in men. When women shovel, they generally clear the narrowest path that will permit safe

passage. Men may start with the same goal, but they usually keep going, ignoring cold feet, aching backs, and even chest pain until every last flake is out of the way. Testosterone has no place on snow-covered driveways.

It's not a small problem. Each winter, more than twelve hundred cardiac deaths occur in the United States during or after snowstorms.

No one with heart disease should shovel snow. Healthy men older than forty-five should do their best to avoid it, as should healthy women older than fifty-five. If you insist on shoveling, play it safe. Warm up before you go out, and cool down afterward. Dress warmly; it's particularly important to protect your feet, hands, and head. Stay well hydrated. Pace yourself and take frequent breaks. Use the principle of high reps and low resistance; it's far safer to lift three light loads than one heavy shovelful, and pushing snow aside is better yet. Avoid heavy, wet, icy snow. Set reasonable goals and stick with them. Clear only the snow that matters; the rest will melt. Your goal is safe passage, not neighborhood honors.

While you are protecting your heart, remember to take care of your back. Bend from your knees, not from the waist. Turn to face the pile instead of twisting your back as you pivot to toss the snow. Carry your load to a low pile instead of straining to heave it onto a high mound.

Above all, listen to your body. Even with careful preparation and planning, snow shoveling can cause problems. Nip small woes in the bud before they become big ones. Put down your shovel and head for home if you experience chest pain, palpitations, undue shortness of breath, fatigue, light-headedness, or nausea—all potential signs of cardiac distress. If your symptoms are severe or if they persist after you've stopped shoveling, contact your doctor without delay.

Pain in your fingers, toes, earlobes, or nose could signal frostbite, and numbness in these areas is even more worrisome. Back pain speaks for itself, or it should.

Snow shoveling is as American as baseball and apple pie, but it's a lot more dangerous. If you must shovel, use extreme caution and care. Better yet, hire a teenager with a shovel or a plow driver. Americans love to avoid exercise, and in this case it's the right thing to do.

Musculoskeletal Injuries

In a perfect world, medications would never produce side effects, operations would always be successful, and the best movie would win the Oscar. In that world, *The No Sweat Exercise Plan* would top the bestseller list, and exercise would continue to prevent disease and prolong life without causing any aches and pains. For better or worse, perfection can never be achieved in the real world. It's a wonderful world and exercise is wonderful for health, but people who exercise do run a risk of injury. One example: a study of 6,313 adults who exercised regularly found that 21 percent developed an exercise-related injury during the course of a year. Two-thirds of these injuries involved the legs; the knee was the most frequently injured joint.

It sounds grim, but it's not. For one thing, injuries are much more common with intense exercise and competitive sports than with moderate exercise of the No Sweat variety. For another, people who exercise actually have a lower long-term risk of disability than sedentary people. A thirteen-year study of 370 exercisers aged fifty to seventy-two, for example, found that exercise was linked to a reduced risk of disability and a lower death rate, even among elderly folks who engaged in running, a high-impact activity.

Injuries do occur, but many are preventable, most are mild, and the majority will respond nicely to simple treatment at home. An old runner's adage boasts, "I have two fine doctors, my right leg and my left." For injury treatment, though, you'll also need your head and your hands. Check the tips at the end of this chapter to learn how to prevent injuries. Listen to your body to detect problems early, when you can treat them yourself. Here is a guide to some common exercise-induced woes:

- **Sprains.** Injuries to ligaments, the fibrous connective tissues that connect one bone to another. In *first-degree sprains*, the ligament is stretched; in *second-degree sprains*, some fibers are torn; in *third-degree sprains*, most or all of the fibers are torn. In general, first-degree sprains produce only pain and swelling, second-degree injuries are often accompanied by weakness and bluish discoloration due to bleeding, and third-degree sprains produce severe weakness and decreased mobility.
- **Strains.** Injuries to muscles or tendons, the fibrous tissues that connect muscles to bones. Commonly known as muscle pulls, strains also come in first-, second-, and third-degree varieties. Like sprains, strains are usually caused by a misstep or fall that places excessive force on a tendon, muscle, or ligament so that fibers are stretched or torn.
- **Tendinitis.** Inflammation of a tendon, often caused by overuse or poor body mechanics. Pain is the major symptom, but warmth, swelling, and redness may occur. The pain is typically most severe at the start of exercise; it eases up during exercise, only to return with a vengeance afterward.
- **Fasciitis.** Inflammation of the layer of fibrous tissue that covers many muscles and tendons. Overuse is often to blame. A common example is *plantar fasciitis*, inflammation of the sole of the foot, which plagues many walkers and runners.
- **Bursitis.** Inflammation of the small fluidlike sacs that cushion joints, muscles, or bones like miniature shock absorbers.
- **Arthritis and synovitis.** Inflammation of a joint (*arthritis*) or the membrane that surrounds it (*synovitis*). Like bursitis, joint inflammation often occurs without being triggered by exercise, but both problems can also result from overuse or trauma. Pain and swelling ("water on the knee," for example) are common symptoms.
- **Dislocations.** Out of joint. Often very painful and disabling, dislocations occur when bones slip out of their

proper alignment in a joint. A deformity is often visible, and the joint is unable to move properly. Although some athletes attempt to realign (*reduce*) a dislocation themselves, it should be done by a physician or highly experienced trainer or physical therapist.

■ **Fractures.** Broken bones. A disruption in the continuity and integrity of a bone. Except for broken toes and *stress* (hairline) *fractures*, nearly all fractures require skilled medical management.

■ **Contusions.** Black and blue marks. Bleeding into tissues caused by direct trauma.

■ **Muscle cramps and spasms.** The charley horse. Unduly strong and sustained muscle contractions that can be very painful. Gentle stretching will help relieve cramps; hydration and good conditioning will help prevent them.

■ **Lacerations and abrasions.** Cuts and scrapes. Small ones can be managed with soap and water and bandages, but larger ones may require special dressings or sutures. Tetanus shots are not necessary if immunizations have been kept up to date with boosters every ten years.

Home Treatment: The PRICE Is Right. Use a five-point program to handle your injuries. The key is PRICE: protection, rest, ice, compression, and elevation.

■ **Protection.** Injured tissues must be protected against further injury. Protect your small injuries by applying bandages, elastic wraps, or simple splints. Something as simple as taping an injured toe to its healthy neighbor can do the job. See your doctor for problems that require precision splints or casts.

■ **Rest.** Injured tissues need time to heal. It's an obvious principle, but once you're hooked on exercise, you may be tempted to ignore it. Don't give in to temptation—you'll shortchange yourself with shortcuts. But you can rest *selectively*; you may have to give up tennis while your serving shoulder recovers from tendinitis, but you can still walk, jog, or hike. In a curious way, an injury is often a blessing in disguise, forcing you to diversify your workouts and acquire new skills.

- **Ice.** It's the cheapest, simplest, yet most effective way to manage many injuries. Ice is an excellent anti-inflammatory, reducing swelling and pain. For best results, apply an ice pack for ten to fifteen minutes as soon as possible after an injury. Repeat the ice treatment each hour for the first four hours and then four times a day for the next two to three days. Protect your skin with a thin cloth, and don't allow your skin to become red, blistered, or numb. After forty-eight to seventy-two hours, switch to heat treatments, using the same schedule and principles.

- **Compression.** Pressure will help reduce swelling and inflammation. In most cases, a simple elastic bandage will suffice; it should be snug but not too tight. Remember that swelling may develop slowly hours after your injury, so you may have to loosen your wrap. Another trick is to place a small piece of foam rubber directly on the injured area before you wrap it; this will allow you to put gentle pressure where it's needed without constricting an entire joint or limb.

- **Elevation.** It's a simple strategy that enlists the force of gravity to drain fluid away from injured tissues, reducing swelling, inflammation, and pain. Keep your sore foot up on a hassock, or put a pillow under it in bed; elevating an injured area will help you get back to earth faster.

Home Treatment: Medication. PRICE is the key to the early management of most kinds of injuries, but you may also need medication for pain or inflammation. *Acetaminophen* (Tylenol and other brands) may be the best choice for the first day or two, since it will reduce pain without increasing bleeding. After that, consider aspirin or other *nonsteroidal anti-inflammatory drugs* (NSAIDs), such as *ibuprofen* (Advil and other brands) or *naproxen* (Aleve), to fight inflammation as well as pain. NSAIDs can irritate the stomach; take them with milk or food, and always follow directions.

Home Treatment: Rehabilitation. Your pain is gone and your swelling is down, but your treatment is not yet over. It's now time to plan your rehabilitation and return to exercise with the same care that you used to treat your injury. As a rule of thumb, give yourself two days of rehab for each day of inactivity due to injury. Start with gentle range-of-motion exercises, and then gradually increase your weight-bearing activities. When you are comfortable, consider building up your tissues with graded resistance training using calisthenics, light weights, elastic bands, or resistance equipment. If all goes well, you can be stronger than before your injury, thus reducing your risk of reinjury. Don't neglect stretching exercises to improve your flexibility. Use heat or massage to warm up your injured tissues before you start your rehab exercises; afterward, apply ice to the area to reduce inflammation. The judicious use of aspirin or other NSAIDs may also facilitate your rehabilitation program.

You can manage many injuries yourself, but don't be stubborn. If you have a major injury—or if your nagging woes don't clear up—get help. An experienced exercise buddy who's been there and done that may be all the help you need. A primary care physician should be able to handle 50 to 60 percent of exercise-induced problems, but more difficult issues require orthopedists, physical therapists, and sports podiatrists. In many centers, these specialists come together in sports medicine clinics.

 Precautions

Exercise is a natural function of the human body, and it's naturally good for your health. Once you get in the swing of it, you won't need to remind yourself of all the benefits you're earning as you walk your way to health. And once you understand the simple rules of safe exercise, they, too, will become natural and automatic. These precautions may make exercise seem risky, but it's not. They may make exercise seem complex, but it's simple. And although a checklist of precautions may give exercisers the aura of a chore, it's actually great fun.

Here are sixteen tips that will keep exercise safe for you without blunting your health benefits or personal pleasure:

1. **Be sure your medical checkups are up to date before you begin a new exercise program.** If you have heart disease, high blood pressure, diabetes, peripheral vascular disease, or major cardiovascular risk factors, see your doctor for clearance; additional evaluations, such as an exercise stress test, may be required.

2. **Exercise at an appropriate level.** Start at a low level and build up gradually. Walk before you run—and remember that as far as health is concerned, walking will do very nicely. Make moderate exercise your goal; go beyond only if you enjoy extending yourself, are healthy enough to push on, and understand how to do it properly and safely. Do what's right for you, not your friends or relatives—especially if they are younger.

3. **Plan a well-rounded program.** Emphasize cardiometabolic activities, but save time to exercise for strength, flexibility, and, if necessary, balance.

4. **Warm up before you exercise and cool down afterward.** Stretching and light calisthenics are ideal warm-up and cooldown activities, as is leisurely walking. Stroll before you walk, walk before you jog, and jog before you run.

5. **Drink plenty of fluids.** When it's warm and muggy, you'll need to replace the large amounts of fluid lost in sweat, and when it's cold and dry, you'll lose a surprising amount from your lungs. Water is an excellent choice.

Drink six to eight ounces for each thirty minutes of moderate exercise, more if it's hot or humid. Dehydration will make you tired and grumpy, and in severe cases, it can make you quite ill. Drink enough so your urine is clear and copious after exercise, but don't go to extremes. If you want to be precise, weigh yourself before and after exercise, without those sweaty clothes, of course. Each pound that you lose will require sixteen ounces of fluid to keep you fully hydrated.

6. **Don't eat within two hours of moderate or intense exercise.** The simple act of digesting food makes your heart work harder to pump blood to your intestinal tract; don't ask it to pump extra blood to your muscles at the same time.

7. **Exercise regularly.** Unless you are ill or injured, try to do it nearly every day. Alternate harder and easier workouts, particularly as you move up the exercise ladder. Vary your activities to keep your muscles fresh and to keep yourself from getting bored or stale.

8. **Don't exercise if you are ill.** Take a break if you have a fever, muscle aches, or flulike symptoms. A simple upper respiratory tract infection, such as the common cold, needn't put you on the shelf, but fever or symptoms below the neck do call for caution and restraint. Don't fail to resume exercising when you recover, but give yourself time to work back to your usual level. As a rule of thumb, allow two days of progressively returning to normal for each day you missed due to illness.

9. **Rest injured tissues.** Often, though, you can find a way to stay active by switching to another form of exercise; if you've sprained an ankle, try using your arms and trunk or exercise in water so you can keep moving without putting weight on your ankles. Rehab your injury so you can get back to normal as soon as possible, but remember that older people take longer to heal.

10. **Use good equipment, especially good shoes.**

11. **Dress appropriately, aiming for comfort, convenience, and safety rather than style.**

12. **Use good technique.** Walking and daily physical activity seem so natural that you may overlook little flaws that may lead to injury. Consider lessons or coaching for sports that emphasize skill and coordination.

13. **Respect the environment.** Adjust your activity, clothing, and diet to cope with heat, cold, or high altitude. Don't risk your neck on the ice or snow, and don't risk your life outdoors in a lightning storm. Develop a menu of exercises so you can stay active in any climate, indoors or out.

14. **Remember that exercise is portable.** Keep active when you are traveling, but adjust your routine in response to local environmental conditions and cultural norms.

15. **Exercise safely.** It makes little sense to reduce your risk of heart attack and stroke by increasing your risk of accidental injury or death. If you walk or jog, always face the traffic. If you bike, ride with the traffic, but always wear a helmet and obey the rules of the road. Avoid heavy traffic and hazardous terrain. If you are out when it's dark, stick to well-lighted streets or paths, and always wear light-colored clothing with prominent reflectors. If you venture off the beaten path, go with a companion and take a cell phone. Avoid rough neighborhoods. Women should be particularly careful of other humans, and all humans should be careful of dogs and other animals.

16. **Above all, listen to your body.** Be especially alert for warning signals of heart disease, including chest pain or pressure; disproportionate shortness of breath, fatigue, or sweating; erratic pulse; dizziness; light-headedness; or even unusual nausea or indigestion. Fainting is particularly worrisome. If you develop any of these symptoms, stop

17

exercising and get help promptly. If you feel better with just a minute or two of rest, a call to your doctor may suffice as the first step toward an evaluation. But if your symptoms persist, call 911 instead. And if you think you may be having a heart attack, chew down an aspirin tablet and stay quiet until help arrives.

Fortunately, serious symptoms are uncommon. But you should also be alert for warning symptoms of dehydration, overheating, or cold weather injury as detailed earlier. And don't ignore aches and pains that may signify injury. Competitive athletes may pride themselves on playing through pain, but ordinary mortals should back off and start the simple treatments that will often prevent more serious problems and speed your return to full activity.

Listen to your body, and listen carefully. Respond forcefully to sounds of discord. But if you respect your body and exercise appropriately, regularly, and properly, you are likely to hear the sounds of harmony and good health.

With just a little care, exercise will be music to your ears.

Going Beyond

CHAPTER 10

Exercise as Therapy

Good for What Ails Many

Good health is a priceless asset. To retain that asset, healthy people should make exercise part of a comprehensive program of prevention that also includes good nutrition and regular medical care (see Chapter 12). Unfortunately, however, many people lack good health—and as our population grows older, the burden of chronic disease continues to increase. Can exercise help people who have already fallen ill? Hippocrates thought so: "Walking is a man's best medicine."

 ## Low-Tech Exercise Versus High-Tech Medicine

Exercise can help treat many chronic illnesses. But just as exercise is often overlooked for prevention, it is widely neglected as a form of therapy. It's a reflection of the high-tech orientation shared by contemporary physicians and their patients. Exercise is time consuming and it seems hard, even risky for people with major illnesses. Medication, on the other hand, is easy to take and reassuringly modern. René Dubos explained the paradox nicely: "To ward off disease or recover health, men as a rule find it easier to depend on healers than to attempt the more difficult task of living wisely."

It's not a question of either/or. People with medical conditions often require both lifestyle and pharmacological treatments. Exercise can help treat some of the most common chronic illnesses in America today, but it often requires special precautions and supervision to be safe and effective.

What common ailments respond to exercise—and what forms of exercise are best?

Coronary Artery Disease

Virtually all patients with coronary artery disease need medication. The goals of drug therapy include improved cholesterol, blood pressure, and blood sugar levels; a reduced risk of artery-blocking blood clots; better arterial elasticity and function; enhanced pumping capacity of the heart muscle; and relief from stress and depression. Exercise can help attain all these benefits for cardiac patients. Most will need medication as well, but many can cut their dosages, reducing the risk of side effects and lowering costs.

When the Harvard Cardiovascular Health Center and other cardiac rehabilitation programs began prescribing exercise for heart patients in the 1970s, the idea seemed radical, even dangerous. In fact, rest had been a mainstay of treatment ever since the heart attack epidemic gathered steam in the early twentieth century. All of that has changed. Unless certain complications are present, doctors and nurses encourage heart attack patients to start walking as soon as they are stable. Most can walk out of the hospital in just three to five days. And these days, many walk back to the hospital eight to ten weeks later to begin supervised exercise for rehabilitation and prevention.

Most programs prescribe walking or jogging on a treadmill or pedaling a stationary bike for thirty to forty-five minutes three times a week. The patients' exercise intensity depends on the results of their stress tests; most aim for 55 to 75 percent of their maximum heart rate, but over time, some progress to long-distance running. Stretching exercises are standard for careful warm-up and cooldown periods. And now that cardiologists know that strength training is safe for the heart and good for the body, most programs prescribe light weight lifting two to three times a week. In addition, patients also receive advice about nutrition and stress reduction. Needless to say, all participants also continue to get individualized cardiological care and medication.

Is exercise safe for heart attack survivors and patients with angina? It is, providing they follow simple precautions. The first requirement is an exercise stress test. Next, they need an individual exercise prescription to prevent overdoing it. Ideally, patients should be supervised by medical personnel as they begin walking to recovery, and they must become expert at monitoring themselves and recognizing warning signals so they can avoid problems when they are ready to exercise on their own. Under these circumstances, exercise is indeed safe. According to a 2005 scientific statement of the American Heart Association, cardiac rehabilitation programs experience only one cardiac death for each 750,000 hours of exercise; that's a lower fatality rate than for people without known heart disease.

Is cardiac rehabilitation effective? A 2004 review analyzed forty-eight randomized clinical trials that compared exercise plus standard medical care with medical care alone in 8,940 cardiac patients. As compared with the best medical care alone, exercise was associated with a 26 percent reduction in the risk of death from heart disease and a 20 percent reduction in the overall death rate.

Cardiology has come a long way, and many patients with coronary artery disease benefit from procedures that actually restore blood flow to the heart muscle by opening blockages with a catheter (*balloon angioplasty*) or bypassing the blockages surgically (*coronary artery bypass graft*). Does exercise therapy have a role when artery-opening treatments are also available? Studies from Italy and Japan tested the value of exercise in patients who had undergone successful angioplasties. The patients who were randomly assigned to exercise therapy plus medical care had better cardiac function and work capacities, fewer cardiac events, a lower hospital readmission rate, and a better quality of life than patients who received standard care without exercise.

Exercise therapy provides additional gains to patients who have already benefited from artery-opening therapy—but can it substitute for high-tech treatment? In some cases, at least, it can. In 2004, doctors in Germany reported the findings of a study of 101 men with coronary artery disease. Half were randomly assigned to receive angioplasties with stents; the others received exercise training that consisted of twenty minutes on a stationary bicycle every day. At the end of twelve months, the exercise patients demonstrated better cardiac function and work capacity. They also had a significantly lower rate of cardiac events (12 percent versus 30 percent)—and because they had fewer hospitalizations and repeat procedures, they also consumed fewer health care dollars.

Exercise is not a panacea for patients with coronary artery disease, but it can be an important adjunct to the high-tech medical and surgical care that overshadow it today. In fact, exercise therapy is an older form of treatment. In 1772 Dr. William Heberden, the great English physician who first recognized angina for what it is, wrote of a patient whose chest pain was "nearly cured" by sawing wood for thirty minutes a day.

Exercise therapy for coronary artery disease may be old, but it should not be old hat.

Congestive Heart Failure

When a solemn cardiologist tells a woman that her husband has heart failure, she's likely to assume she's already a widow. That's because many people, male and female, confuse heart failure with *cardiac arrest*, the complete cessation of the heart's function. Congestive heart failure (CHF) is entirely different. It's a chronic condition in which the heart keeps on pumping, but it's not pumping well. CHF is an extremely serious condition in its own right. And since some 4.7 million Americans have CHF, it's a big problem for all of us.

The most common causes of CHF are coronary artery disease and high blood pressure. Exercise can help prevent both, but it won't do much against other causes, like heart valve disease and heart muscle disease. In most cases, CHF develops gradually. The major symptoms are fatigue, general weakness, shortness of breath, and fluid accumulation. At first, breathlessness and fatigue occur only with moderate exertion, but as CHF progresses, they come on with even mild activity and then at rest. New medical therapies, which typically involve combinations of five types of drugs, have greatly improved the outlook for patients. But even with the best medications, lifestyle therapy is crucial. One key element of lifestyle therapy, a low-sodium diet, has stood the test of time, but the other has not.

Bed rest is a traditional treatment for CHF, but new research has turned the old dogma upside down. Rest may help in the short term, but exercise is better in the long run. Exercise may help improve the heart's pumping capacity, and it surely helps muscles use oxygen more efficiently, so they get more mileage from the blood they receive. Regular exercise also helps blunt some of the body's excessive responses to CHF, especially when it comes to blood vessel function. For example, a recent six-month study of seventy-three men with CHF demonstrated that modest exercise slowed the heart rate, increased the amount of blood pumped with each beat, and boosted exercise tolerance—and all it took was twenty minutes a day of stationary bicycling.

Patients with advanced CHF cannot exercise, but those with mild to moderate symptoms can—and should. No Sweat exercise is best, but never to the point of breathlessness or discomfort. Stationary biking or a daily walk of twenty to thirty minutes complemented by very light weight training several times a week seems ideal. CHF patients should get medical clearance and direction before they begin. It's one of the new approaches that have brought so much hope to tens of thousands suffering from this debilitating and threatening condition.

Hypertension

High blood pressure is a major risk factor for coronary artery disease and congestive heart failure, to say nothing of stroke, kidney failure, mental deterioration, and visual loss. Exercise can also help treat the sixty-five million Americans who have hypertension. Many randomized clinical trials have demonstrated that it can lower systolic and diastolic blood pressure by an average of 7.4 mm Hg and 5.8 mm Hg, respectively. No Sweat exercise, such as walking, is best; more intense activities do not appear to produce further reductions in pressure. Low-resistance weight training also helps treat hypertension. And as in primary prevention, exercise treatment works best when combined with other lifestyle interventions.

American physicians have not done a good job at diagnosing and treating hypertension. About a third of patients with high blood pressure don't know they have the condition, and about two-thirds of diagnosed patients are not being treated adequately. Walk down to your medical facility to find out if you have hypertension, walk to the drugstore to get any medications you may need, and keep walking to help lower your pressure.

Peripheral Artery Disease

Cholesterol-laden plaques that block the coronary arteries can cause angina and heart attacks. Similar plaques in the arteries that carry blood to the brain can cause strokes. Plaques in the arteries of the lower body are the culprits in peripheral artery disease (PAD).

PAD gets less attention than the other, more dramatic manifestations of atherosclerosis. That's small comfort to the nine million Americans with PAD. In mild cases, they suffer leg cramps that limit walking (*intermittent claudication*); in severe cases, they suffer pain at rest or tissue damage that can lead to amputation.

All patients with PAD should be treated for the underlying problem, atherosclerosis. That means avoiding tobacco and controlling cholesterol, blood pressure, blood sugar, body weight, and other risk factors. Severe PAD requires angioplasty or bypass surgery to restore the blood supply. But mild to moderate claudication usually responds well to noninvasive therapy.

Unfortunately, medication is only marginally helpful. Still, a good treatment is available. Paradoxically, perhaps, the most important treatment for intermittent claudication is the very thing that triggers the leg pain: exercise. The most successful regimen begins with supervised exercise training, typically in thirty- to sixty-minute sessions three times a week. Although walking is the mainstay of treatment, many programs mix in biking, stair-climbing, and resistance exercise. In most cases, patients who can walk only fifty to a hundred yards before developing pain can walk two or even three times farther at the end of twelve weeks of training—and if they continue exercising on their own, they can expect still more improvement over the next year or so.

Exercise will not cure PAD, but for many patients with intermittent claudication, it will feel that way.

Diabetes

The bad news is that some sixteen million Americans have diabetes and their numbers are growing every year. The good news is that many new medications are available to control the disease. The unreported news is that exercise is an effective form of therapy.

Exercise lowers blood sugar levels in patients with diabetes. Nine trials report an average drop of about 20 mg/dL, enough to make a real difference. Even more important, exercise reduces complications of the disease. A recent study of 2,896 diabetic adults, for example, found that patients who walk for one to two hours a week enjoyed a 39 percent lower mortality rate than sedentary patients, and those who walked three to four hours a week benefited from a 54 percent drop in the death rate. And in this research from the Centers for Disease Control and Prevention, walking at a moderate pace appeared more beneficial than intense exercise.

The No Sweat program is ideal for diabetics, but they require special precautions. The first issue is cardiac risk, particularly in patients who have had diabetes for ten years or more. Diabetics should obtain medical clearance for exercise; exercise stress tests may be helpful.

The second concern is that exercise may produce hypoglycemia, an abnormally low blood sugar level, in patients who are taking insulin or other sugar-lowering medications. In particular, patients on insulin should monitor their own blood sugar levels and should anticipate a reduced need for the medication on days they exercise. A small preexercise snack can help, and patients should carry candy to boost blood sugar levels if they develop symptoms of low blood sugar during exercise. A medical alert bracelet may provide additional protection, and patients should try to avoid injecting their insulin in a limb that will be exercised. Finally, diabetics who exercise should pay particular attention to foot care, since they may have nerve damage that reduces their sensitivity to injury and tissue damage.

Do the benefits of exercise warrant these extra precautions? You bet. And since all diabetics should already know to pay meticulous attention to their blood sugar levels, medications, and diets, these simple guidelines should be as natural as exercise itself.

Arthritis

Exercise makes joints work. Arthritis makes joints hurt. People with arthritis should not exercise. The reasoning is clear—but it is also wrong. Exercise can actually help many people with arthritis if they exercise a little extra care.

About eight million Americans have arthritis that is severe enough to produce some degree of disability, and tens of millions have a milder form of the disease. Although there are many forms of arthritis, the vast majority of patients have *osteoarthritis*. It is commonly referred to as "wear-and-tear" arthritis, but its true cause is unknown. Osteoarthritis does become more common with advancing age, but most scientists no longer believe that simple overuse is the culprit. Contrary to popular belief, in fact, even high-impact exercises, such as running, do not cause clinically significant arthritis, though sports injuries that damage joints do increase risk.

Exercise can help patients with osteoarthritis and some other less common forms of chronic arthritis. Once again, the No Sweat approach is ideal. Cardiometabolic exercise (see Chapter 4) helps improve general health. It also helps patients lose weight, a particularly good thing for painful joints, and it builds endurance, which is particularly important for people who find that the normal activities of daily life require extra effort and energy. Low-impact exercise is best. Swimming and other aquatic exercise provide cardiovascular conditioning and flexibility training without the stress of weight bearing. Walking and biking are also desirable, as are elliptical trainers and rowing machines (see Chapter 11).

Stretching exercises (see Chapter 6) help keep joints flexible. A stretching routine should always include healthy joints, since they face extra stress as patients compensate for the limitations of arthritic joints. Finally, resistance exercises (see Chapter 5) are very important, not only for general health, but to strengthen muscles so that they take some of the load off joints.

Randomized clinical trials show that exercise helps patients with osteoarthritis and rheumatoid arthritis. People are rewarded for their efforts by a reduction in joint pain, increased mobility, and greater ease and comfort with the activities of daily living. Exercise helps patients with arthritis fend off disability.

People with mild arthritis can plan their own exercise program using the guidelines in Chapters 4 through 8 and the precautions in Chapter 9. They should be particularly careful to warm up before exercise; many people feel that applying a heat pack to arthritic joints before exercise helps reduce stiffness and pain. The cooldown is equally important, and an ice pack can do wonders here. Leave yourself extra time to build up your exercise level, and listen to your body with added attention. If you have any concerns, get professional guidance. And individuals with moderate or advanced arthritis should get personal instruction and supervision from doctors and physical therapists.

Exercise was first recommended for joint and muscle pain more than three thousand years ago, and it remains a useful adjunct to therapy in our new millennium.

Stress

The mind and body are inseparable aspects of the human organism. In Chapter 1, I reviewed the ways in which bodily exercise helps keep the mind healthy. But exercise can also help restore emotional well-being to people whose psychic equilibrium is out of balance.

The body's response to mental stress is very similar to its response to physical stress. That's because it is a fundamental—and normal—human response to threat. In the early years of the twentieth century, Dr. Walter B. Cannon of Harvard Medical School pioneered the medical study of the fight-or-flight reaction. Stress produces a state of arousal. The mind becomes more vigilant, and the pupils widen to admit more light. Breathing speeds up, and the bronchial tubes widen to admit more oxygen. The heart beats faster and pumps more blood, raising the blood pressure. Blood is directed away from the intestinal tract and the skin, which feels cold and clammy. More blood is delivered to the muscles, which become tense and ready to spring into action.

Stress also affects the body's metabolism. *Adrenaline* and *cortisone* are pumped into the blood. In contrast, insulin levels fall and blood sugar rises to provide instant energy to the brain, heart, and muscles. And the blood itself changes, as the clotting system is activated to staunch any wounds.

Stress can be good or bad for health. If it helps you get pumped up to meet a challenge, it's a plus. But if it is triggered inappropriately, is unduly severe, or is excessively prolonged, it's harmful. Excessive stress produces exhaustion—and illness.

Although anxiety and stress may feel very similar, there is an important difference. Stress is the body's response to an external threat, but anxiety is the response to an internal stimulus. Stress may be helpful or harmful, but anxiety is always unpleasant and unwelcome. Exercise can help dissipate stress and anxiety. And it can also help lift the spirits of people afflicted with an opposite set of symptoms, the lethargy, sadness, and pessimism of depression.

Various studies show that exercise can help people cope with stress, anxiety, and depression. In some studies, the results are quite remarkable. For example, doctors from Duke University and the University of California performed a randomized clinical trial that found exercise as effective as *sertraline* (Zoloft, a powerful antidepressant) for treating major depression in 156 older men and women. And a 2004 observational study of depressed cardiac patients reported that physical exercise was linked to a reduced risk of recurrent heart attacks and a lower overall mortality rate. Most investigations have focused on cardiometabolic activities such as walking, but people who perform stretching or strength training also often report mental improvements.

Scientists don't know exactly how physical exercise helps improve mental well-being. Many factors seem to contribute. Fit individuals have lower heart rates and adrenaline levels. Exercise boosts *endorphins*, the body's painkilling, opiate-like chemicals. Purely psychological effects such as a sense of accomplishment, self-discipline, optimism, and mastery also play a role. Enhanced energy and vigor help, too. Individual exercise gives people an opportunity to get away from it all and enjoy peace and solitude, while shared activities provide companionship and help build social support networks.

"All men," wrote Aquinas, "need leisure." Exercise is play and recreation; when your body is busy, your mind will be shielded from the pressures of daily life and will be free to think creatively.

Stress control does not occupy a block in the No Sweat Exercise Pyramids, but it is a flag that can be attached when needed (see Chapter 8). One of the major benefits of cardiometabolic exercises, such as walking or swimming, is the rhythmic, repetitive action of major muscle groups. It's a sort of "muscular meditation," with many similarities to mental meditation.

Even fitness fanatics can use a little extra help with stress control from time to time. You can help yourself with autoregulation techniques, such as deep breathing, progressive muscular relaxation, and meditation. Professional help is also available. But for most of us, the key is balance.

Just as a balanced program of moderate exercise is crucial for physical health, a balanced life is crucial for mental health. Balance exercise with rest, work with play, discipline with indulgence. Balance stimulation and challenge with relaxation and recovery, excitement with calm. Balance independence with interdependence, solitude with companionship. Balance practical realities with hopes and expectations, effort with relaxation, routine with spontaneity. Balance your needs with those of your family and community.

Balance your mind and body to keep both active, healthy, and happy.

Chronic Fatigue

Exercise provides healthy people with extra energy and vigor. Can it also help rehabilitate patients who are disabled by chronic fatigue?

Chronic fatigue syndrome is the ultimate challenge. It is a common, still mysterious condition dominated by disabling fatigue that persists for six months or longer in the absence of an underlying physical cause of exhaustion. Other symptoms may include headaches, disturbed sleep, muscle and joint aches, chilly sensations, malaise, and tender lymph glands.

Despite intensive investigation, the cause of chronic fatigue syndrome remains unknown. Most experts believe that a variety of abnormalities act in concert to produce the symptoms.

Because doctors don't know what causes chronic fatigue syndrome, they have not discovered a specific therapy. Many treatments have been tried, but only one has been consistently effective: exercise. For example, a 2004 Australian trial randomly assigned sixty-one patients to a progressive exercise program or a relaxation and flexibility program. The exercisers walked, swam, or biked every second day. Because they were so deconditioned and tired, some started with as little as five minutes of exercise and then worked slowly up. At the end of twelve weeks, the exercise group improved significantly, but the relaxation group did not. And similar programs have helped patients with related conditions, such as postmenopausal fatigue and fibromyalgia. Gentle exercise can also boost the energy levels of patients suffering from the fatigue of cancer and cancer therapy.

Too tired to exercise? Don't bet on it.

 ## Exercise as Medicine

Exercise can help improve various aspects of health in a remarkably broad range of illnesses. In addition to the major conditions discussed in this chapter, smaller studies have reported benefit in patients with problems ranging from cystic fibrosis to stroke, chronic kidney failure, Alzheimer's disease, and advanced physical frailty in the elderly. And in terms of overall benefit, a Minnesota study of 2,336 adults with chronic diseases linked physical activity to a more than 50 percent reduction in the mortality rate, even after age, smoking habits, functional status, and the severity of illnesses were taken into account. For all its benefits, though, exercise requires special precautions and supervision in people with major illnesses—and it should always be used to supplement, not supplant, the best medical and surgical treatments that are available.

The seventeenth-century poet John Dryden proclaimed, "The wise, for cure, on exercise depend." Exercise therapy has, of course, lost its primacy in the modern era, but today's doctors should be well versed in its very real benefits.

Exercise diligently to help preserve good health. Exercise carefully to help restore damaged health.

CHAPTER 11

Beyond Health

Exercise That Makes You Sweat

n Chapter 2, I explained that the human body has a minimum daily requirement (MDR) for exercise, just as it has for nutrients. Using the CME point system developed in Chapter 4, the MDR for good health is 150 points a day, or about 1,000 points a week. That level of activity will provide wonderful health benefits. You'll gain a bit more by racking up 250 to 300 points a day, particularly when rapid weight loss is a goal.

You can get the exercise you need without pushing yourself hard enough to break into a sweat. Thirty to forty minutes of moderate exercise nearly every day will meet your MDR for health. But as you get into shape and see what exercise has done for you, you may be tempted to go beyond the minimum, to exercise for fitness, sports, and the sheer pleasure of exercise itself.

You can extend your horizons simply by logging more No Sweat exercise or by increasing the intensity of your activity. Either way, be sure not to let the extra exercise harm your health. A study of 5,001 adults who exercised at the Cooper Aerobics Center found that intense exercise carries a higher risk of injury than moderate exercise. Still, you can reduce your risk with a few precautions. Don't skimp on warm-ups or cooldowns. Stretch diligently. Build up gradually. Alternate hard or long workouts with moderate or shorter ones. Plan a variety of activities to keep your mind and your muscles fresh. Above all, listen to your body with extra attention.

Let's look at some ways you can exercise the No Sweat way for health or at perspiration intensity for fitness and sports.

Exercise Machines

The human body is a magnificent machine for exercise; although many have tried, no engineer has designed a better one. But machines can allow the human body to exercise in the privacy of a home or the gung-ho atmosphere of a health club.

Exercise machines offer many advantages. A single device can be used for moderate or intense exercise as well as for low-level warm-ups and cooldowns. By switching machines, you can exercise different parts of your body. Although some require a little instruction and practice, exercise machines don't demand skill or athletic experience. When used correctly, they pose a low risk for injury. Since they can be installed at home, machines are very convenient, efficient, and time saving. They also make daily exercise possible in hostile weather.

As is true of the human body, the most important problem is disuse. The stationary bike is an example; it's an excellent tool for cardiometabolic exercise, but too often it features two pedals, one seat, and no rider. Good intentions alone won't get you good health; for that, you'll have to exercise. Boredom is the main barrier. To help maintain your motivation, listen to music or watch TV or videos while you exercise. You can read while pedaling a bike, and you can read with your ears while using any machine. Recorded books are great for motivation—particularly if you resist the temptation to finish the tape in your car or den, so you'll have to get on your treadmill or elliptical to find out how the story ends.

Exercise machines have two other drawbacks: they can take up lots of space and they can be expensive. To conserve space, some families buy machines that fold for storage. It's a fine idea, but it usually flops: folding machines are often less sturdy than stationary models, and the extra effort of hauling a machine out of storage is the dagger in the heart of motivation. Another common solution to the space dilemma is to set up the machine in an out-of-the-way place, such as a basement, an attic, or a garage. That's another bad idea. Out of sight is out of mind. Put your machine in a convenient, pleasant location that will help make exercise enjoyable. If your space is limited, choose a compact device, such as a climber or bike, instead of a larger machine, such as a treadmill or rower.

The expense factor can also be overcome. The trick is to favor function over form. Look for a sturdy machine with adjustable intensity settings and one that fits you comfortably. Electronic bells and whistles run up the bill, but unless you need them for motivation, they're entirely optional. In general, you'll be wise to choose a stripped-down utilitarian machine made by a reputable manufacturer specializing in fitness equipment. And you can also save a lot of money by purchasing a pre-owned machine; in most communities, they are easy to find through newspaper ads and community bulletin boards, and, I'm sorry to say, many are in mint condition, owned but not used.

Which machine is best for you? Don't let infomercials choose for you. Instead, try out various models at a fitness store, health club, or Y. If possible, use them several times each before you write a check. Look for a machine that's easy to use but still challenging and enjoyable. For many people, a treadmill is best, but if you already walk or jog outdoors, you might decide to diversify by buying a stationary bike or stair-climber. On the other hand, if your passion is cross-country skiing or rowing, you might pick a machine that simulates these sports so you can extend your short season and stay in shape the year round. To help you decide, here's a brief guide to the basic machines.

Stationary Bikes

Long the workhorses of exercise programs, stationary bikes have many advantages: they are compact, durable, quiet, and relatively inexpensive. Upright bikes are more compact, but some people find recumbent bikes more comfortable. Most will exercise only your leg muscles, but dual-action upright bikes have handlebars that permit simultaneous arm exercise. Standard exercise bikes use flywheels for resistance; a heavy wheel will give you smoother action. Other models use air paddles for resistance; you'll get a cooling breeze that may encourage you to keep pedaling.

Look for a sturdy bike with a comfortable, well-padded seat. One-piece pedals with stirrups are best. Pick a machine with smooth pedaling action and precise controls that allow you to vary the resistance level.

Treadmills

Walking is the most natural form of exercise. A treadmill will allow you to walk or run at home; you'll miss the scenery, but you'll also miss the summer's smog and the winter's worst. Treadmills allow you to select and vary your speed; better models also allow you to vary the incline as you walk or jog.

Most people find it easier to use a treadmill than other exercise machines. Their drawbacks are size and cost. If you have the floor space, look for a midpriced model with a sturdy frame and a strong, quiet motor. Your treadmill should have simple controls that allow you to vary the belt speed easily. Models that permit you to vary the incline while you are walking are also desirable.

Cross-Country Ski Machines

Nordic skiing is among the most demanding of aerobic sports; ski machines can bring the challenge home—without the snow. Cross-country ski machines have the advantage of working your arms and back as well as your legs. Because they produce little impact, they cause few injuries. People who are athletically inclined may find skiers more stimulating than other some home machines. But they do require more balance and coordination, and they tend to take up more space than stationary bikes or climbers.

Machines that have skis that glide independently, cables for your arms, and flywheels for resistance provide better action than models with linked ski motions, poles, and pistons. Look for a sturdy frame and for controls that allow you to set your arm and leg resistance separately.

Rowing Machines

Like ski machines, rowers have the advantage of exercising more than just your legs; they also exercise your arms and torso. You can get a fine, low-impact workout, but you'll need some floor space, and you'll need good technique to avoid back injuries; instruction can help. Models with cables for "oars" and flywheels for resistance give a more authentic feel than rowers with handles and pistons. Look for a stable frame and a comfortable seat that glides smoothly.

Stair-Climbers

Stair-climbing is an excellent, strenuous way to condition your heart and your legs. That's why competitive athletes run stadium steps and dancers do step aerobics. Climbing machines have soared in popularity since their introduction in 1985. They offer moderate or high-intensity exercise with low impact. Most models exercise legs only, but dual-action climbers have "ladders" for arm exercise.

Because of their expense, motorized climbers are more suitable for clubs than for home use. But piston climbers are affordable and compact. Look for a sturdy frame, large pedals, and a comfortable handrail. Above all, your climber should have smooth action and easily adjustable resistance settings.

Exercise Riders

Spurred by televised promotionals, riders were the rage of the 1990s. As on a rower, you pull with your arms and push with your legs—but on a rider, you lift your body up instead of sliding it forward as on a rower. Riders have the advantage of exercising your arms and legs without impact. Look for a stable machine with a comfortable seat, smooth action, and variable resistance settings.

Elliptical Trainers

What do you get if you cross a bike, a stair-climber, and a cross-country skier? With a good designer and a little luck, you'll come up with the latest word in exercise machines, an elliptical trainer. To use an elliptical, you stand on footplates while grasping handlebars. As you walk or run, your feet move in an elliptical fashion; as one moves forward and up, the other moves down and back—it's halfway between the circles your feet make on a bike and the vertical motions they make on a climber. At the same time, you can move your arms against resistance, as you would on a ski machine.

Elliptical trainers provide moderate to intense low-impact workouts for your legs and, to a lesser degree, your arms. You can vary the intensity by adjusting the resistance and incline; better models also allow you to pedal backward to give your buttock muscles some extra work.

Because they are new and sexy, ellipticals tend to be expensive, and they do take some getting used to. They are more suitable for moderate to intense exercisers than beginners. Look for broad, nonslip pedals, comfortable handlebars, and a smooth, easy-to-adjust mechanism.

Home Gyms

All the exercise machines discussed thus far are designed mainly to provide cardiometabolic exercise. But you can also purchase home gyms for strength training. They use cables and pulleys to guide weights so you can exercise most of your major muscle groups. Home gyms are bulky and the best models are expensive. For moderate strength training, free weights and/or elastic bands will do just fine at a much lower cost.

Health Clubs

Groucho Marx once said that he'd never join any club that would accept him as a member. Any health club will accept you, and most will try to induce you to sign up for a long-term membership. But should you be a Groucho or a joiner? Is a health club right for you?

Benefits

A health club can provide three major benefits: motivation and companionship, instruction and supervision, and equipment and facilities.

Motivation is the most important benefit, especially for people who are just starting to exercise. The first steps to fitness are the hardest. It can take two to three months to get hooked on exercise; going to a club can make those initial workouts easier to take. For many, paying up front also provides motivation, since the only way to get your money's worth is to show up.

Instruction is another major benefit, both for beginners and for people who are ready to move to a new level. Most clubs offer free hands-on guidance to get you started on a piece of equipment, and many offer personal trainers to plan and supervise an individualized regimen, usually for an extra fee. Group classes are often available, providing companionship, motivation, and instruction all at once.

A third reason to join a club is to get your hands—or feet—on the equipment there. Home exercise equipment is great, but few homes can accommodate more than one or two devices. Every health club will have treadmills, bikes, stair-climbers, ellipticals, resistance machines, and weights, and some have more, even swimming pools.

Picking a Club

Exercise facilities range from old-fashioned, unadorned gyms to fancy clubs and sleek spas. Here are some tips to help you find the club that's best for you:

- Look for a club that's convenient. If at all possible, pick a club within ten to fifteen minutes of your home or work. Location is everything, or at least nearly everything.
- Be sure the club is open when you want to use it and that it's not too crowded at your favorite times.
- Be sure the club has what you want, but don't pay for more than you need. If you're a treadmill, bike, and Nautilus type, you can save big bucks by staying away from clubs that have racquetball courts and steam rooms.
- Check out the atmosphere. Intangibles can make or break a club. A club should be inviting—clean, bright, and upbeat. It should also be compatible with your personality and style.
- Give the club a checkup. Choose one that's appropriate for your age and health. A good club should ask you to fill out a medical questionnaire, possibly including an OK from your doctor. If you have medical problems, find a club that has the equipment and personnel to provide first aid.
- Check out the staff. Are they just bodybuilders who look good, or are they well-trained fitness experts? A good credential is certification by an organization such as the American College of Sports Medicine, the National Academy of Sports Medicine, the American Council on Exercise, or the Aerobics and Fitness Association of America.
- Ask if the club offers supplementary services, such as child care or sessions on nutrition, injury prevention, stress management, and weight control. Ask, too, if there is an extra fee for these programs.
- Talk to club members to find out how they like it. Be sure to ask if the club delivers on its promises.
- Ask for a free introductory workout or an inexpensive trial membership, the best way to see if the club works for you.

- If you travel often, try to find a club that offers reciprocal memberships with facilities in other cities.
- Join an established club that's unlikely to close suddenly, leaving you with a prepaid invitation to a locked building.
- Read the contract, even the fine print.
- Evaluate the payment options. A monthly or quarterly fee will give you more security than a prepaid annual fee. Ask if there is a finance charge. Pay with a credit card if you can, just in case your club fails to deliver what it promised in your contract. Look for specials or negotiate your own deal.
- Sign the shortest contract you can, particularly if it's your first health club membership. Try to find a plan that will allow you to opt out for a small charge or one that you can sell to a friend for a modest transfer fee.

In a sense, a health club is just a big, expensive piece of exercise equipment. If you use it, you'll feel great and enjoy many health benefits, but if not, you'll just feel guilty and wasteful.

 ## Personal Trainers

It's the twenty-first-century route to fitness. A fit, energetic, enthusiastic young man or woman meets you at home or at a gym to get your body in shape. It's the latest trend in fitness, but are personal trainers just a passing fad, or can they really help build fitness and enhance health?

Benefits

A good trainer should be able to provide help in five areas:

- **Making assessments.** In the first session, the trainer should evaluate your starting points, including endurance, strength, and flexibility. Most trainers will also evaluate your body fat and weight. Many will discuss nutrition; although this may be helpful, it's very important to remember that trainers are not professional nutritionists. All responsible trainers will ask about your medical history and previous or current injuries to be sure your exercise program will be safe.

- **Establishing goals.** Are you interested primarily in health? Weight? Physical appearance? Athletic performance? The trainer should understand your aims and help establish realistic goals.
- **Providing instruction.** Once you know where you want to go, the trainer should show you how to get there. Good technique will help prevent injuries.
- **Monitoring progress.** The trainer should help you establish a system to see how you are doing in each target area.
- **Providing motivation.** Perhaps the most important thing a trainer can do is to keep you moving toward your goals, especially when you are just beginning a fitness program. By providing a schedule, setting expectations, and offering encouragement and enthusiasm, a personal trainer gives you the same intangibles that a good coach brings to his or her team.

Practicalities

Anyone can claim to be a trainer, but not everyone should.

Because trainers are not licensed, there are no standards that assure qualified instruction. A personal recommendation, therefore, is the best way to find a trainer. Health clubs will often make referrals. But remember to interview the trainer before you sign up. Certification by organizations such as the American College of Sports Medicine, the National Academy of Sports Medicine, the Aerobics and Fitness Association of America, or the American Council on Exercise is important. Certification means that a trainer has attended a two- to four-day course and has passed an exam. You should also check whether a trainer has liability insurance. Finally, evaluate a trainer's personality and style; since motivation is a primary reason for using a trainer, good chemistry between you and the trainer is essential.

You can use a trainer in many ways. For some people, one or two sessions will be enough to get an exercise program going. More often, follow-up sessions are part of the plan. You can see your trainer once a month or once a week, but folks who really need hands-on guidance (and can foot the bill) may try to have a trainer at most workouts. But in the final analysis, the only trainer who really matters is you. A personal trainer can push and prod, but your muscles have to do the work that will earn such rich rewards in fitness and health.

Sports and Recreation

You can get the exercise you need with the simple, balanced No Sweat program. But sports and games can also be a wonderful way to health, adding zest and variety and providing camaraderie, challenge, and, for those who seek it, competition.

Just as walking is the mainstay of No Sweat exercise, running is the poster child of intense exercise. Let's jog through some basics about running and then run through a few highlights of some other games people play.

Jogging and Running

It's true that you should always walk before you run. But it's also true that you should consider running before you move on to other intense sports.

Like walking, running is entirely natural. Naturally enough, the two share many advantages. Like walking, running requires little in the way of skill and technique. A good pair of shoes is the only essential equipment you'll need, but high-tech running suits are great assets in cold or wet weather. The cost of running is low, and the convenience and flexibility it affords are very high. Like walking, running can provide solitude or companionship, indoor exercise or outdoor activity, recreation or competition.

The only difference between jogging and running is pace. In my younger days, I used to say that I was running, but slower folks were jogging; now that the shoe is on the other foot, I'm less concerned about the distinction. But at any pace, running does have a more fundamental difference from walking. Whereas walkers have one foot in contact with the ground at all times, runners are entirely airborne for some time during each stride. As pace increases, moving from jogging to running to sprinting, the percentage of the stride that's airborne increases; competitive runners have "flight times" of about 45 percent.

Why run if you can walk for fitness and health? The faster pace of jogging and running adds efficiency. A 150-pound person will earn 80 CME points in a mile of walking or a mile of running, but walking that mile may take fifteen minutes, jogging ten or twelve minutes, and running seven or eight minutes. You can fulfill your weekly exercise quota faster with running than with walking. The extra intensity of running can be both challenging and enjoyable; the longer distances you can travel in an hour also allow you to really "go places."

Another advantage of running is that it's an excellent conditioning activity for other sports. Participants in other endurance sports, such as biking and cross-country skiing, don't need to run because they can use their own sports for conditioning, but people who enjoy tennis, basketball, baseball, soccer, and other team and competitive sports really should run to train for top performances at their favorite games.

If running will provide all the benefits of walking in less time, why shouldn't everyone run? The extra intensity of running increases the risk of injury. Unlike walking, running is a high-impact exercise. It's simply a matter of gravity: what goes up must come down. Airborne runners return to earth with each stride, putting a stress equal to eight times their body weight on their feet, legs, hips, and necks. In just one mile, a runner's legs will have to absorb more than one hundred tons of impact force; it's a testament to the wonderful construction of the human body that it can be done with relatively few problems. But the faster the pace, the greater the impact and the greater the risk of injury. That's why only 1 to 5 percent of walkers report exercise-related injuries, while runners face a 20 to 70 percent risk, depending on how careful they are (and how honest they are about reporting injuries).

With care, jogging and running can be safe and enjoyable. The main rules are familiar: start slowly, build up gradually, alternate harder and easier workouts, and listen to your body and heed its messages. Here are a few details:

- **Wear good shoes.** Shop as you would for walking shoes (see Chapter 4), but this time buy a pair specifically designed for running, not walking. Change your shoes every three hundred to four hundred miles; even if they don't look worn, they will have lost crucial cushioning and support.
- **Don't run on uneven or slanted surfaces.** Find the most forgiving surfaces available; asphalt is softer than concrete, and packed dirt or grass is better still.
- **Even if you feel terrific, don't increase your distance by more than 10 percent a week.** You can bite off more than you can chew with your feet as well as your mouth. Don't be tempted to do too much too soon.
- **Vary your pace.** Always warm up with stretching exercises before you start out, then walk and jog before you run. Don't try to sustain a rapid pace; instead, throttle down and coast a bit from time to time. And always slow down to a walk at the end of your run.
- **Be careful on hills.** Going up hills requires lots of extra effort; expect to slow down and lean into the hill. Don't try to sprint down; to avoid injury, shorten your stride and hold back. Remember the old runner's motto: uphills train, downhills maim.
- **Unless you are entered in a race, don't race.** And even in a race, remember there is always someone faster (also smarter, richer, thinner, and better looking—that's life). Stay within yourself; if you know your limits, your exercise won't be limited by injury. As usual, Shakespeare got it right: "Too swift arrives as tardy as too slow" (*Romeo and Juliet*).

- **Follow the same rules for safety, hydration, and climate as advised for walkers (see Chapters 4 and 9).** But remember, you'll generate more heat and lose more fluid in sweat when you run.
- **Do extra stretching for the muscles and tendons of your legs, especially your hamstrings, calves, and the others at the back of your legs.** Running makes these muscles strong but tight.
- **Don't run through pain.** Return to walking (unless that hurts, too). Treat yourself with rest, ice, compression bandages, and (if needed) anti-inflammatory medications, and build back up when you're better. If problems linger, see a physical therapist, sports podiatrist, or sports-minded physician (usually an orthopedist).

Even with precautions, many runners develop inflammation, strains, and sprains that produce aches and pains in tendons, muscles, or ligaments. Most are mild, and all will resolve with time and treatment. But can running also cause permanent joint damage or arthritis? Most nonrunners would answer yes, but most studies of runners say no. Repetitive use, such as long-distance running, has been linked to a slight increase in x-ray abnormalities, but not to an increase in clinical osteoarthritis (unless a significant injury has occurred along the way). Contrary to expectations, in fact, runners actually have fewer musculoskeletal complaints over the years than inactive folks. A California study of 498 long-distance runners found they had fewer aches and pains and less disability than their age-matched sedentary peers.

Running is not for everyone. But if you are interested in making the transition from walking to running, a model training schedule is available at health.harvard.edu.

Cross-Country Skiing

For runners, *snow* is a four-letter word—unless they take up skiing. Although downhill skiing is much more popular, cross-country skiing is far superior for fitness. Unlike downhill skiing, cross-country skiing is superb for aerobic training; it also provides excellent muscular conditioning for the arms, back, and trunk as well as the legs. As a low-impact sport, cross-country skiing causes few overuse injuries. Accidents are less common and less serious than they are on the downhill slopes. Cross-country gear is less expensive than downhill equipment; still, it makes walking shoes or swim goggles look like a bargain.

Rowing

Like cross-country skiing, rowing is an esoteric endurance sport—not when you use your father's dinghy, but when you use a modern rowing shell. It rivals cross-country skiing in its splendid attributes: superior cardiovascular conditioning, balanced muscular development, low impact, and few injuries. But although rowing ranks among the very best fitness exercises, it ranks last for practicality. Rowing requires very expensive equipment, a stretch of calm, uncrowded water, and a moderately difficult technique.

Aerobic Dance

Long familiar as a performing art, a social skill, and a romantic recreation, dance took its proper place as a fitness activity in the 1970s. Dance has two important advantages: it provides a unique brand of companionship and camaraderie that can help motivate regular participation, and it conditions all major muscle groups. Dance injuries can be minimized by careful stretching and warm-ups, high-quality aerobic shoes, good leadership and instruction, and resilient dance floors. Low-impact dance techniques are particularly desirable.

Skating

Ice-skating, roller-skating, and, the newest craze, in-line skating, are all excellent endurance activities. They can be used to build aerobic fitness, to condition leg muscles, to have fun, and to compete. They do require equipment that can be expensive, and they demand moderate levels of skill and coordination. Falls and accidents also must be counted among the drawbacks of skating. Still,

TABLE 11.1 A Comparison of Sports

Endurance Activities	CME Benefits	Legs	Arms	Back and Trunk
Walking	Moderate	Moderate	Low	Low
Running	High	High	Low	Low
Swimming	Moderate to high	Moderate	High	High
Biking	Moderate to high	Moderate	Low	Low
Aerobic dancing	Moderate to high	Moderate	Moderate	Moderate
Cross-country skiing	High	High	Moderate	Moderate
Rowing	High	High	High	High

Team Sports and Games of Skill	CME Benefits	Legs	Arms	Back and Trunk
Golf	Low (riding)/ moderate (walking)	Low	Low	Low
Bowling	Low	Low	Low	Low
Basketball	Moderate	Moderate	Low	Low
Downhill skiing	Low	High	Moderate	Low
Soccer	Moderate	High	Low	Low
Softball	Low	Low	Low	Low
Tennis	Moderate	High	Moderate	Moderate

skating is a low-impact sport that glides nicely into a balanced fitness program.

Team Sports and Games of Skill

Many competitive and team sports can be useful for health as well as for play. But few offer enough flexibility, efficiency, and balance to serve as the core of your exercise program. Don't count on competitive sports to get into shape. Instead, use endurance sports or exercise machines to get into good cardiometabolic condition. Add the flexibility and strength training you need. Then use your multifaceted fitness to play for fun as well as for health. Table 11.1 compares some aspects of popular sports.

So many sports, so little time. But so many opportunities to expand your exercise options. Stick with the basics for health, but expand your repertoire if you are tempted. Experiment with a variety of activities, learn new skills, meet new people, and have fun—all in the name of wellness.

CHAPTER 12

Beyond Exercise

Nutrition and Preventive Medical Care

What is a chapter on diet and doctors doing in an exercise book? *The No Sweat Exercise Plan* is not about exercise for sports or fitness but about exercise for health. And while moderate exercise is essential for optimal health, it is not sufficient. Together, inadequate exercise and poor diets account for some 360,000 unnecessary, premature deaths in the United States each year. To stay well, you need to avoid both hazards—and you need just a little help from your doctor in the form of preventive maintenance. That's why nutrition and medical care each occupy a block in the No Sweat Exercise Pyramids (see Chapter 8).

Like exercising regularly, following a good diet may require some lifestyle changes and discipline at first—but like exercise, a good diet will become enjoyable, automatic, and natural in a short time. It's no surprise, since in both cases you'll just be going back to basics, returning to the natural lifestyle that best fits the human genetic endowment.

If you exercise regularly, you'll gain a lot of flexibility and wiggle room in your dietary decisions. You'll also need fewer trips to your doctor. Now that you're in the know about exercise, let's review the essentials of a good diet and the preventive medical checkups that can help healthy people stay that way.

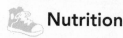 **Nutrition**

Exercise and nutrition are the hand and glove of preventive medicine. It's a crucial concept, but it's hardly a new insight. In 400 B.C., Hippocrates wrote, "Eating alone will not keep a man well; he must also take exercise. For food and exercise, while possessing opposite qualities, yet work together to produce health. For it is the nature of exercise to use up material and of food and drink to make up deficiencies."

How far have we come from the Greek ideal? In today's world, the Mediterranean diet remains closest to and is a fine model for healthful eating. But the typical American diet is not. Some twenty-four hundred years after Hippocrates, Harvard Professor John Kenneth Galbraith observed that "more die in the United States of too much food than of too little." Although he is an economist, the good professor was right. As a nation, we are consuming far more calories, fat, cholesterol, refined sugar, animal protein, sodium, and alcohol than is healthful—and we are also getting far less fiber and complex carbohydrates and far fewer vitamins than we should.

What are the elements of a good diet?

Calories

Diet impresarios to the contrary, calories do count; people who consume more calories than they burn up will gain weight, but those who achieve the reverse will reduce. As a rough guide, a sedentary person needs about thirteen calories per pound of body weight each day to maintain a steady weight; moderate physical activity boosts the daily quotient to sixteen calories per pound, vigorous exercise to eighteen calories a pound each day. On average, then, a 120-pound woman who consumes fifteen hundred to twenty-two hundred calories a day will keep her weight stable, as will a 170-pound man who takes in between twenty-two hundred and thirty-one hundred calories.

The caloric value of nutrients varies considerably: carbohydrates and proteins have four calories per gram, alcohol has seven, and fats pack nine calories per gram. Because it is so calorie dense, dietary fat is the most potent nutritional determinant of body weight.

Fat and Cholesterol

First came the bad news: as the average American's consumption of fat and cholesterol increased during the twentieth century, our risk of heart attack and stroke also rose to record levels. Next came the good news: eating less fat and cholesterol can reduce that risk. It's true and it works, but it's not the whole story. In fact, scientists are now learning that there are important differences among the dietary fats; many are living up to their reputation as villains, but a few may prove to have a positive, if not heroic, effect on health.

Nearly all the fats in the human diet are absorbed into the body in the form of fatty acids. Although each fatty acid has unique properties, they fall into several major families that produce characteristic effects on health. Animal fats are high in *saturated fatty acids*, as are four vegetable oils (see Table 12.1); most other vegetable oils contain *unsaturated fatty acids*. In broad terms, saturated fatty acids raise blood cholesterol levels and increase the risk of heart disease, while unsaturated fats do not. But new research indicates that it's not quite so simple; in fact, the unsaturated fatty acids are themselves quite diverse. The best of the best are the *omega-3 polyunsaturates*, especially the two found in fish oil. Close behind are the *monounsaturates*; olive oil, still a staple in the Mediterranean diet, is an excellent source. Most vegetable oils contain omega-6 polyunsaturates, which appear to be neutral in terms of blood cholesterol levels and health. But the *trans fatty acids* found in partially hydrogenated vegetable oils are the worst of the bad; like most saturated fats, they raise LDL ("bad") cholesterol levels, but they also possess the uniquely harmful ability

TABLE 12.1 The Fats in Foods

Saturated Fats

Animal	Vegetable
Dairy fats	Coconut oil
Meat and poultry	Cocoa butter
Tallow	Palm oil
Lard	Palm kernel oil

Trans Fatty Acids

Margarine
Fried foods
Commercial baked goods
Snack foods
Puddings

Monounsaturated Fats (Omega-9)

Omega-9
Olive oil
Canola oil
Safflower oil (hybrid)
Sunflower oil (hybrid)

Polyunsaturated Fats

Omega-6	Omega-3	
	Fish	Vegetable
Corn oil	Mackerel	Canola oil
Safflower oil (regular)	Tuna	Walnut
Sunflower oil (regular)	Salmon	Flaxseed
Soybean oil	Sardines	Rapeseed
Cottonseed oil		Wheat germ
		Soya seed

Cholesterol

Dairy products
Egg yolks
Meat (especially organ meats, fatty and prime cuts)
Poultry (especially the skin)
Shellfish (especially shrimp)

to reduce HDL ("good") cholesterol levels. Trans fats are man-made and are found in many processed foods.

Cholesterol is not a fatty acid but a *sterol*, a waxy substance with a complex ringlike structure. Cholesterol is present only in

TABLE 12.2 The TLC Diet

Total calories	Adjusted in conjunction with exercise to attain or maintain healthy body weight
Total fat	25–35% of total calories
Saturated fat	Less than 7% of total calories
Polyunsaturated fat	Up to 10% of total calories
Monounsaturated fat	Up to 20% of total calories
Cholesterol	Less than 200 mg a day
Carbohydrates	50–60% of total calories
Fiber	20–30 g a day
Protein	About 15% of total calories

animal tissues. The body can make all the cholesterol it needs; that's why strict vegetarians stay healthy even though their diets contain no cholesterol at all.

How much fat and cholesterol should you consume? The therapeutic lifestyle changes (TLC) diet proposed by the National Cholesterol Education Program Expert Panel provides sound guidelines for healthy people; it also proposes standards for some other nutrients that will be discussed shortly (see Table 12.2).

Guidelines are important, but they won't get you very far at restaurants and food markets. To turn from the forest to the trees, read food labels with care and visit the Harvard Health Publications website (health.harvard.edu/no_sweat).

Just as health-conscious Americans were learning to replace harmful dietary fats with carbohydrates, a new controversy erupted: diet books and talk shows are demonizing carbs as the true agents of heart disease and obesity.

What's a person to do? The answer is not a return to fat or a flight to protein. The right choice is still carbohydrates. But to exercise that choice healthfully, you must understand that, like fats, not all carbs are alike. In general, carbohydrates that are slowly absorbed and raise the blood sugar slowly are more healthful than those that boost sugar levels rapidly.

Dietary carbohydrates come in three varieties: simple carbohydrates, complex carbohydrates, and fiber. Despite many important differences, simple and complex carbohydrates all have the same energy value: four calories per gram. It's one of the nice things about carbs, which are less calorie dense than alcohol (seven calories per gram) or fat (nine calories per gram). Because fiber is indigestible, it has virtually no caloric value—but it certainly has lots of health value.

Simple sugars are the least desirable carbohydrates: they are absorbed quickly and they are empty calories, lacking other nutrients. Unfortunately, average Americans get about 20 percent of their calories—about half their total carbohydrate intake—from simple sugars. That's a lot of sugar, amounting to about 160 pounds a year for the typical adult. And America seems to have an insatiable sweet tooth; sugar consumption doubled between 1900 and 2000, and the rise shows no signs of slowing.

You don't have to forswear all sweets to be healthy, but you should limit your consumption of simple sugars to less than 10 percent of your total caloric intake. For the average adult, it works out to about fifty grams of sugar a day; that's about twelve teaspoons of table sugar, hardly a Spartan ration.

Complex carbohydrates are a big step up nutritionally. Because they must be broken down into simple sugars before they're absorbed, they raise the blood sugar slowly. And when complex carbohydrates are present in unrefined foods, they are accompanied by vitamins, minerals, and other valuable nutrients. In addition, unrefined foods are filling, so it's harder to overdose on them.

If you succeed in reducing your consumption of simple sugars to 10 percent of your day's calories, make up the difference by increasing your complex carbohydrates to 40 to 50 percent.

Dietary fiber is a special type of complex carbohydrate. Found only in plants, the best sources of fiber are the bran of whole grains, the stems and leaves of vegetables, and fruits, seeds, and nuts. Although there are many types of fiber, they all belong to one of two broad categories, soluble and insoluble. Both are important for health, but soluble fiber has special benefits for the metabolism: it slows the absorption of other carbohydrates so that blood sugar levels rise more gently, and it helps lower LDL ("bad") cholesterol levels, resulting in a lower risk of heart disease and diabetes. Even without these benefits, insoluble fiber is a health asset because it increases the water content of feces, making the stools bulkier and easier to eliminate. The result is a reduced risk of diverticulosis, hemorrhoids, hernias, and even colon cancer.

The TLC diet recommends twenty to thirty grams of fiber a day, but new studies suggest thirty to thirty-five grams a day may be even better. Visit health.harvard.edu/no_sweat to get a detailed look at the sources of dietary fiber. When it comes to choosing carbohydrates, favor those that are absorbed into the blood slowly (having a low *glycemic index*, or GI) over those that are rapidly absorbed (with a high GI). The GI may sound complex, but its lesson is simple: favor unrefined, coarsely ground foods over highly processed foods. Here are some examples:

Instead of	Consider
White bread	Whole grain bread
Cream of Wheat	Oatmeal
Corn Flakes	All-Bran
White potatoes	Yams
White rice	Brown rice, beans, or pasta
Fruit juice	Fruit
Tropical fruits, such as bananas	Temperate-climate fruits, such as apples

For a look at the glycemic index of your favorite foods, visit health.harvard.edu/no_sweat.

Protein

Without enough dietary protein, the body's tissues will weaken. If the deficiency is severe or prolonged, the body will break down its own proteins faster than they can be rebuilt. The result is tissue wasting and weakness that are most notable in the body's most protein-rich tissue, muscle. Fortunately, dietary protein deficiency is very rare in developed countries; average Americans, for example, get more than twice as much protein as they need.

Can too much of a good thing be harmful? The answer for dietary fat and carbohydrates is yes, for protein, maybe.

Protein has four calories per gram, exactly the same as carbohydrates. Although the body does not store excess calories as protein, it can and does convert the carbon, oxygen, and hydrogen from amino acids into fats, which always seem to pile up where they're least welcome. Popular theories notwithstanding, proteins are fattening.

Fat has no nitrogen. What becomes of the nitrogen from excess dietary protein when it's stored away as fat? It is excreted in the urine, but that's not the end of the story. In fact, for the kidneys to excrete extra nitrogen, they have to work extra hard. In animals, long-term protein excess leads to enlarged kidneys and premature aging of these vital organs. Doctors don't know if the same thing occurs in humans, but they do know that patients can slow the progression of certain kidney diseases by reducing the amount of protein they eat.

As nitrogen enters the urine, it carries calcium and sodium along with it. The extra urinary calcium can increase a person's risk of osteoporosis and kidney stones. On the other hand, the sodium loss is a good thing, explaining why high-protein diets appear to lower blood pressure.

Healthy people should get about 15 percent of their daily calories from protein; that's about 0.36 grams per pound of body weight. Here's how it rounds out:

Body Weight (in Pounds)	Daily Protein Requirement (in Grams)
100	36
120	43
140	50
160	58
180	63

Men above 180 will do quite well with sixty-three grams (two and a quarter ounces) of protein per day. Athletes may be an exception; since they have larger muscles that are working harder, they may benefit from a 20 percent increase in daily protein. Women who are pregnant or lactating should add about thirty grams a day. Higher amounts are perfectly safe in the short run, though they may have adverse effects in the very long run.

Unless you have special problems, such as advanced kidney disease or liver disease, you don't have to count up the proteins in your diet. A balanced diet will give you all the protein you need, and if you keep your dietary protein to about 15 percent of your total daily calories, you won't get too much. To help guide you, visit health.harvard.edu/no_sweat to view the protein content of various foods.

Water

Water is present in all the body's tissues; it accounts for about half of a person's weight. Because water is required for all the body's processes, you need about a quart of water for each thousand calories you burn. For most people, that means an intake of about two quarts a day, but it doesn't all have to come from beverages. In fact, about 60 percent of the body's needs are met by the water contained in food. In ordinary circumstances, just a pint and a half of water will make up the difference.

If you are healthy, thirst is a reliable guide to your fluid needs, and you don't need to force down the eight glasses of water a day that are often recommended. But remember to take in extra water when you exercise (see Chapter 9). Air travel, hot weather, fever, and diarrhea also call for extra fluids.

Vitamins

Vitamins are organic (carbon-containing) molecules that are required for many of the body's metabolic processes. Because the body cannot manufacture them, vitamins must be consumed on a regular basis. All thirteen vitamins are essential nutrients. Only tiny amounts are needed to prevent vitamin-deficiency diseases, but slightly larger amounts of certain vitamins may provide additional benefits.

A good diet will give you all the vitamins you need—with one important exception. The only meaningful dietary sources of vitamin D are milk and fish. Government regulations require manufacturers to add vitamin D to milk. Each eight-ounce serving should contain 100 IU, but many brands contain less. And even with full fortification, you'd have to drink a quart of milk to get 400 IU of vitamin D. Considering that people between the ages of fifty and seventy should get 400 IU a day and older people 600 IU a day, that's a lot of milk. Although fish also provides vitamin D, you'd have to eat five ounces of salmon, seven ounces of halibut, thirty ounces of cod, or nearly two cans of tuna to get 400 IU.

Although it is possible to get enough vitamin D from your diet, it is quite difficult. It is part of the case for a daily multivitamin. A multivitamin will also provide insurance that you are getting enough of the other vitamins you need; B_6, B_{12}, and folic acid are particularly important. Look for an inexpensive brand providing 100 percent of the daily reference intakes. "All-natural" vitamins don't offer additional benefits, and "high-potency" preparations may do more harm than good. Extra antioxidants are not beneficial. For more information about vitamins, visit health .harvard.edu/no_sweat.

Minerals

Minerals are chemically the simplest of nutrients, but their roles in the body's metabolism are complex. At least sixteen minerals are essential for health; details are available at health.harvard.edu/ no_sweat. Three are important—and controversial—enough to review here: sodium, potassium, and calcium.

Sodium. Sodium has been every bit as controversial as vitamins; in this case, though, the controversy is even more intense in the scientific community than in the general public. The reason: sodium is the key mineral in salt, and scientists have been divided about the role of salt in causing high blood pressure. Finally, though, consensus is emerging. Here are four key facts that nearly all researchers agree about:

1. Some people are clearly very sensitive to sodium and can reduce their blood pressure significantly by reducing their salt consumption. Other people are less sensitive but can improve their blood pressure with other dietary adjustments (increased potassium, calcium, and fiber from fruits, vegetables, and nonfat dairy products) and lifestyle changes (exercise, weight control, prudent alcohol use, and stress control).

2. The average American diet contains much, much more sodium than is necessary. The average person gets more than four thousand milligrams of sodium a day, or about the amount in two teaspoons of table salt; that's more than four times the amount the body needs to keep its fluids in balance.

3. Salt is not part of a natural human diet. Only small amounts are present in fresh foods, but large amounts are added to processed foods. Average Americans get only 10 percent of their dietary sodium from the natural content of foods, another 15 percent tumbles from the salt shaker, while 75 percent is added to food during the commercial manufacturing process.

4. Salt is an acquired taste, and, over time, people can reacquire a natural taste for low-sodium foods. Slow change is the key; sodium-free seasonings, such as pepper, lemon juice, and various herbs, can help.

Taking all the data about sodium into account, the American Heart Association and the Food and Drug Administration suggest a target intake of 2,400 milligrams a day. The Institute of Medicine proposes 1,500 milligrams as ideal but up to 2,300 milligrams as acceptable. Unless your blood pressure is optimal and stays that way as you age, you should consider adjusting your diet to meet these goals. In most cases, that will mean cutting down on salted snack foods; canned juices; canned and dried soups; prepared con-diments, relishes, and sauces; soy and teriyaki sauces; canned, processed, smoked, and cured meats and fish; frozen dinners; pack-aged mixes for sauces and baked goods; cheese; and, of course, table salt. A detailed list of the sodium content of selected foods is available at health.harvard.edu/no_sweat.

Potassium. Potassium is, in many respects, the opposite of sodium. The two minerals concentrate in different body com-partments; potassium is found in the fluids within cells, sodium in the fluids that bathe cells from the outside. Potassium is found in fresh produce, sodium in processed foods. And diets high in potassium are generally associated with low blood pressure, while high-sodium diets can be associated with hypertension.

Unless you have kidney disease or certain other conditions that may raise your blood potassium levels, you should walk to the mar-ket to stock up on foods high in potassium and fiber; citrus fruits, dates, bananas, raisins, beets, beans, potatoes, broccoli, squash, spinach, and tomatoes are examples. The Institute of Medicine sug-gests a potassium intake of 4,700 milligrams a day; that's about 40 percent more than the average American gets. You'll need to eat five to nine servings of produce and two or more dairy products a day to meet that goal. For details about the potassium content of selected foods, visit health.harvard.edu/no_sweat.

Calcium. Calcium is important to keep bones strong, reducing the likelihood of osteoporosis and fractures. Calcium-rich diets appear to reduce the risk of high blood pressure, but calcium supplements are not effective in treating hypertension. A high intake of cal-cium has been linked to a reduced risk of colon cancer, but very high levels, above 1,500 milligrams a day, may raise a man's risk of prostate cancer. Contrary to long-standing beliefs, dietary cal-cium does not increase the risk of kidney stones, but high doses of supplements may do so, at least in people who are predisposed to stone formation.

Dietary sources of calcium are available at health.harvard.edu. At present, fewer than half of all Americans meet the goal of 1,000 milligrams a day below age fifty and 1,200 milligrams a day after age fifty. You can take supplements of calcium carbonate or calcium citrate to make up for dietary deficiencies, but you need an adequate intake of vitamin D to absorb calcium; a daily multivitamin will go a long way toward providing the necessary vitamin D. Because some studies suggest a very high intake of calcium may increase the risk of prostate cancer, men may be wise to limit their consumption to 1,200 milligrams a day. For details on the calcium content of selected foods, visit health.harvard.edu/ no_sweat.

The Best Diet

We don't dine on polyunsaturated fats, carbohydrates with a low glycemic index, or trace elements—we eat food. Here are twenty guidelines for healthful and enjoyable eating:

1. Eat a variety of foods. Since no single food is perfect, you need a balanced mix of foods to get all the nutrients you need.
2. Eat more vegetable products and fewer animal products.
3. Eat more fresh and homemade foods and fewer processed foods.
4. Eat less fat and cholesterol. Fat should provide 25 to 35 percent of the calories in your diet. Restrict saturated fat to less than a quarter of your total fat intake by reducing your consumption of meat, whole dairy products, and the skin of poultry. Limit your intake of trans fatty acids by reducing your consumption of partially hydrogenated vegetable oils found in margarine, fried foods, and many commercially baked goods. Favor monounsaturated and omega-3 fats that are found in olive oil, canola oil, and fish. Restrict your cholesterol intake to less than 300 milligrams per day by reducing your intake of egg yolks and other animal products.

5. Eat at least 25 grams of fiber per day by increasing your consumption of bran cereal, whole grains, vegetables, and fruit. Favor oats, barley, beans, and other sources of soluble fiber. Consider fiber supplements if you cannot obtain enough fiber from foods.

6. Eat more complex carbohydrates and less sugar by eating more grain products, starchy vegetables, and pasta. Complex carbohydrates should provide 50 to 60 percent of the calories in your diet. Favor foods with a low glycemic index.

7. Eat protein in moderation. Protein should provide about 15 percent of the calories in your diet. Favor fish, legumes, and skinless poultry as protein sources. Experiment with soy as a protein source.

8. Restrict your sodium intake to less than 2,300 milligrams per day, particularly if your blood pressure is borderline or high, by reducing your use of table salt and processed foods, such as canned soups and juices, luncheon meats, condiments, frozen dinners, cheese, tomato sauce, and snack foods.

9. Eat more potassium-rich foods, such as citrus fruits, bananas, and other fruits and vegetables. Eat more calcium-rich foods, such as low-fat dairy products, broccoli, spinach, and tofu.

10. Eat more grain products, especially whole grain products, aiming for six or more servings per day.

11. Eat more vegetables and legumes, especially deep green and yellow-orange vegetables. Aim for at least five servings of vegetables each day.

12. Eat more fruits, aiming for at least two to four servings each day.

13. Eat more fish, aiming for at least two four-ounce servings per week.

14. If you choose to eat red meats, reduce your intake to about two four-ounce servings per week. Avoid "prime" and other fatty meats, processed meats, and liver.

15. Eat chicken and turkey in moderation, always removing the skin.

16. Eat eggs sparingly, aiming for an average of no more than one egg yolk (including those used in cooking and baking) per day. Use egg substitutes whenever possible.

17. Use vegetable oils in moderation, favoring olive oil and canola oil. Reduce your intake of partially hydrogenated vegetable oils, palm oil, coconut milk, and cocoa butter.

18. If you choose to use alcohol, drink sparingly. Men should not average more than two drinks per day, women one to two a day. Count five ounces of wine, twelve ounces of beer, or one and a half ounces of spirits as one drink. Never drive or operate machinery after drinking.

19. Adjust your caloric intake and exercise level to maintain a desirable body weight. If you need to reduce, aim for gradual weight loss by lowering your caloric intake and increasing your exercise level.

20. Avoid fad diets and extreme or unconventional nutritional schemes. If it's too good to be true, it's not true.

I hope you will consider these guidelines carefully and decide to adopt them. Remember, though, that they are guidelines written on paper, not commandments etched in stone; the fine print is likely to change as doctors learn more about nutrition and health. Remember, too, that they are intended for healthy people. People with medical problems should consult their doctors to develop individualized nutritional plans.

If you decide to change your diet, don't try to reform all at once. It is hard to sweep away a lifetime of habits, so change slowly. Enlist the support and cooperation of your family and friends. Think of good nutrition not as a punishment but as an opportunity to explore new foods and recipes. Experiment creatively. Give your tastes some time to change, and don't be too hard on yourself if you happen to slip up from time to time. It's not the first day that counts—it's the lifetime of days that lie ahead of you.

As you plan your diet, remember to take your personal preferences into account. If roast beef is your favorite food, it is OK to eat it, but try to make it a Sunday treat instead of a daily staple. The choices are yours—and the more you exercise, the more wiggle room you'll have to indulge your passions.

Diet or exercise? For the best health, it's not either-or, but both. And along with some simple health habits, routine medical care will complete your program for prevention.

Preventive Medical Care

Although much has changed over two and a half millennia, modern medicine still traces its roots to the ancient Greeks. Those early physicians attributed health to Aesculapius, the god of healing. But Aesculapius, however powerful, didn't go it alone; instead, he divided his responsibilities between his two daughters. Hygeia was put in charge of wise living and healthful behavior, while Panacea governed the use of medication.

In this case, as in many others, the Greeks got it right: good health depends on a combination of a healthful lifestyle and effective medical care. I wrote *The No Sweat Exercise Plan* because exercise is one of Hygeia's key mandates, and I've focused on diet

TABLE 12.3 Ten Commandments of Prevention

I	Avoid tobacco and illicit drugs.
II	Exercise regularly.
III	Eat well.
IV	Stay lean.
V	If you choose to drink, limit yourself to one or two drinks a day and drink responsibly.
VI	Avoid excess stress.
VII	Wear seat belts, drive carefully, and behave prudently to avoid accidents.
VIII	Minimize your exposure to radiation, ultraviolet rays, chemical pollutants, and other environmental hazards.
IX	Protect yourself from sexually transmitted diseases.
X	Listen to your body; report distress signals to your doctor, and get preventive medical care.

in this final chapter because it is of equal importance. To hear the music of good health, you need the bow of exercise and the fiddle of nutrition. But there are other players in the orchestra as well. Table 12.3 lists the Ten Commandments of Prevention for you to consider.

You may be surprised to see medical care relegated to tenth place on the list. Indeed, if you take good care of yourself, you'll dramatically reduce your need for medical care. Unfortunately, though, Hygeia is not a panacea, and things may go wrong from time to time. You need a good doctor to take you over the bumps and to coordinate the simple preventive services that are important for even the healthiest of us.

Our health care system is complex, and it continues to be in flux. You should try to stay abreast of developments and work with other professionals for positive reforms. Above all, concentrate on the basics, on the core issues that remain constant in a sea of change: find a good doctor, regularly get the checkups and tests you should have, and understand how to get help when you need it.

Your Doctor

Your doctor is still the key, but he or she is not likely to work alone. Instead, your doctor is likely to share responsibility for your care with other physicians and with nurses and assistants. In this case, more is better, as long as you have a designated individual who is in charge of the team. In most cases, it's a primary care physician; that usually means an internist or a family practitioner, but healthy premenopausal women can substitute a gynecologist who is willing to assume the extra responsibility.

Sharing Responsibilities

Although your primary care physician should be the conductor of your health orchestra, you should remain involved as the general manager. The doctor-patient relationship should be a partnership, with both parties working together to solve health-related problems.

Communication is the key. Not even the best doctor can read your mind. If you have worries or concerns, discuss them. Learn to talk frankly. Be an active, informed health care consumer. Keep lists of your questions, and don't hesitate to ask for a clarification if you don't understand an answer. Don't be afraid to ask a "dumb question." There is no such thing (though there are dumb answers). Don't be surprised if your doctor doesn't know all the answers. Nobody does, and a doctor who thinks he or she knows it all is a bigger worry than one who will try to learn new things to meet your needs. And don't hesitate to ask for a second opinion if you are not satisfied with your doctor's answers.

Keep your own medical records—not all the details, but the dates of important events, the results of major tests, and the effects of treatments. It's particularly important to keep track of your medications. Know what you are taking and why. Check to be sure that drugs won't interact adversely with each other, and find out if they should be taken at a special time of day or if food will affect their absorption. Be sure to inform your doctor and pharmacist about any nonprescription drugs and supplements that you are using. Keep a careful, up-to-date list of allergic reactions and side effects. And take good care of your pills: store them in their original bottles, in a cool, dry, secure place; don't take them if they look or smell funny; and discard them when they expire or you no longer need them.

Stay informed about new developments in medicine. Use books, newsletters, newspapers, and magazines. Surf the Web and visit your favorite health sites regularly. But don't try to be your own doctor. No consumer health product can convey all the complexities and nuances of medicine, and many, unfortunately, don't even try. Check the credentials of your sources, and discuss what you learn with your doctor before you make any big changes.

Preventive Medical Services

Prevention is the best medicine. The best prevention depends on you, not your doctor. Still, your doctor can help. The great Greek physician Galen was among the first to voice the idea when he wrote, "Since, both in importance and time, health precedes disease, so we ought to consider first how health may be preserved, and then how we may best cure disease." But our modern notion of preventive maintenance is much newer; it dates from 1900, when Dr. George Gould articulated the concept that periodic medical care could prevent disease. With automobile maintenance as a model, Americans rapidly embraced the idea of preventive care. That's why the preventive checkup is the single most common reason that people see their doctors, accounting for about five hundred million office visits a year.

During the past thirty years, the old concept of preventive maintenance has taken on a new look. Without disputing the importance of prevention, doctors have been reevaluating the value of specific tests and treatments to find out which are really beneficial. The most comprehensive reviews have been performed by the U.S. Preventive Services Task Force and the Canadian Task Force on Preventive Health Care. In addition, many organizations have issued guidelines of their own. Examples include medical specialty groups, such as the American College of Physicians, and advocacy groups, such as the American Cancer Society, the American Heart Association, and the American Diabetes Association.

With so many people at work, disagreements are inevitable. Fortunately, most disputes relate to details, not principles—and even the best guidelines are subject to change as new data accumulate.

Above all, guidelines are suggestions, not commandments. While valuable, they can and should be adapted to meet individual needs. For example, people at higher risk for a particular disease should have more intensive testing than people at low risk.

Table 12.4 shows suggestions for routine tests and treatments for healthy adults. Except where otherwise noted, they apply to individuals with average risk factors, no symptoms of disease, and normal physical exams. They are based principally on the suggestions of the U.S. Preventive Services Task Force and the American College of Physicians. And, of course, they are subject to modification and change.

TABLE 12.4 Preventive Medical Services for Healthy Adults

Tests and Measurements

For Men and Women

Blood pressure	At every physical exam; at least every 1–2 years.
Body mass index	At every physical exam; at least every 1–2 years.
Cholesterol profile	At the initial checkup; then at least every 5 years.
Fasting blood sugar test	At age 45; then every 3 years.
Complete blood counts	At the initial checkup; then periodically.
Urinalysis	At the initial checkup; then periodically.
Colon cancer screening	Strongly recommended starting at age 50. People at average risk can choose among 4 options: 1. Annual fecal occult blood testing (FOBT) with colonoscopy for a positive test. 2. FOBT as in number 1 plus sigmoidoscopy every 5 years. 3. Colonoscopy every 10 years. 4. Double-contrast barium enema every 5–10 years. Individuals with higher than average risk should choose colonoscopy; examples include people who have had previous colon polyps and those with colon cancer in a parent or sibling.
Electrocardiogram	Baseline at about age 40; then periodically.
Chest x-ray	Not recommended for screening.
Eye exam by specialist	Baseline at age 50; then every 1–2 years.
Hearing tests	Not recommended for screening.
Dental exam	At 6- to 12-month intervals.
Skin cancer screening	Periodic self-examination, with physician exams at regular checkups. Exams by specialists for people at high risk.

For Men

Prostate cancer screening	Annual PSA blood tests and digital rectal exams should be offered to men starting at age 50 (40 or 45 for African-Americans or men with fathers or brothers with prostate cancer). Testing is unlikely to be helpful beyond age 70.
Testicular cancer screening	Periodic self-examination, with physician exams at regular checkups until age 35.
Abdominal aortic aneurysm (AAA) screening	An abdominal ultrasound exam for men between ages 65 and 75 who have smoked or have a family history of AAA.

For Women

Pap test	Every year between ages 20 and 30. Every 1–3 years between ages 31 and 65, depending on previous results, risk factors, and type of test. May discontinue at age 65 if findings have been normal.
Breast cancer screening	Clinical breast exam every 3 years between ages 20 and 40.
Clinical breast exam and mammogram	Every year beyond age 40.

TABLE 12.4 Preventive Medical Services for Healthy Adults, *continued*

Tests and Measurements

Thyroid test	Thyroid-stimulating hormone blood test every 5 years starting at age 50.
Bone density test	Baseline between menopause and age 65 if risk factors are present or by age 65 if no risk factors are present; repeat test every 2 years if abnormal or risk factors are present.

Immunizations

Tetanus diphtheria booster	Every 10 years.
Influenza vaccine	Every fall, starting at age 50.
Pneumococcal pneumonia vaccine	At age 65, with boosters every 5–10 years.
Hepatitis A vaccine	Two injections 6 months apart for travelers to high-risk areas or people at risk for close contact with infected individuals.
Hepatitis B vaccine	A series of 3 injections over 6 months for people at risk of exposure to blood or body fluids.
Immunizations for measles, rubella, polio, yellow fever, cholera, typhoid	Individual recommendations for travelers and others at particular risk.

Considering all the tests and treatments that are available for sick people, the list for healthy people is surprisingly short. To keep your own preventive maintenance simple, you'll have to take good care of yourself. You'll also have to listen to your body; if you detect signs of discord, discuss them with your doctor to see if additional tests may be helpful.

 No Sweat Prevention

Medical screening tests are designed to detect certain illnesses at their earliest, most treatable stages. But imagine for a moment that instead of offering you tests at your checkup, your doctor offered you a magical treatment that could go a long way toward preventing many of these conditions? What if the preventive pill could improve your cholesterol, lower your blood pressure, reduce your weight, and decrease your risk of diabetes, heart disease, stroke, osteoporosis, gallstones, colon cancer, and breast cancer? Taking the pill would also give you more strength and energy, lift your spirits, and reduce the stress in your life. Men would find their prostates working better as they grow older, and men and women would find nearly every part of their bodies aging slowly and gracefully. Your mind would work faster and stay sharper over the years. Best of all, taking the pill would help you live longer as well as better.

Powerful medications are usually costly, and many have serious side effects. Not so our magic pill. It's free for the asking, and it's really quite safe.

Too good to be true, you say. Yes and no. I admit the magic intervention doesn't exist in pill form, and you can't get it from your doctor. In fact, it's not magic, but it is a reality. And if you don't know the name of this miracle of prevention and good health, go back to page 1.

The "magic" of prevention is exercise.

Additional Resources

Exercise is as old as humanity, but medical knowledge is expanding at a startling pace. Even as you stick to the basics, you should stay abreast of new developments.

Harvard Health Publications is an excellent resource (full disclosure: I am a Harvard Health Publications faculty member, and I edit the *Harvard Men's Health Watch* newsletter). Harvard Health Publications publishes monthly newsletters, special reports, and books, and it provides the editorial content for the InteliHealth website. You can learn more about Harvard Health Publications by visiting health.harvard.edu or by calling (800) 829-3341.

The motto of *Harvard Men's Health Watch* is "Knowledge is Power." The newsletter provides knowledge about exercise and nutrition (among other things) for both men and women, as well as information directed specifically toward men (and the women who watch over them). Here are some other sources of information about exercise:

American Academy of Orthopaedic Surgeons
6300 North River Road
Rosemont, IL 60018-4262
(800) 346-AAOS (2267)
aaos.org

American College of Sports Medicine
P.O. Box 1440
Indianapolis, IN 46206
(317) 637-9200
acsm.org

American Council on Exercise
4851 Paramount Drive
San Diego, CA 92123
(800) 825-3636
acefitness.org

American Diabetes Association
Attn: National Call Center
1700 North Beauregard Street
Alexandria, VA 22311
(800) 342-2383
diabetes.org

American Dietetic Association
120 South Riverside Plaza, Suite 2000
Chicago, IL 60606-6995
(800) 877-1600
eatright.org

American Heart Association
National Center
7272 Greenville Avenue
Dallas, TX 75231-4596
(800) AHA-USA1 (242-8721)
americanheart.org

American Physical Therapy Association
111 North Fairfax Street
Alexandria, VA 22314-1488
(800) 999-2782

apta.org

Arthritis Foundation
P.O. Box 7669
Atlanta, GA 30357-0669
(800) 568-4045
arthritis.org

Centers for Disease Control and Prevention
National Center for Chronic Disease Prevention and
    Health Promotion
Division of Nutrition and Physical Activity
1600 Clifton Road
Atlanta, GA 30333
cdc.gov/nccdphp/dnpa

Fifty-Plus Lifelong Fitness (formerly Fifty-Plus
    Fitness Association)
2483 East Bayshore Road, Suite 202
Palo Alto, CA 94303
(650) 843-1750
50plus.org

National Association of Governor's Councils on Physical
    Fitness and Sports
65 Niagara Square, Room 607
Buffalo, NY 14202
(716) 583-0521
physicalfitness.org

National Heart, Lung and Blood Institute
NHLBI Information Center
P.O. Box 30105
Bethesda, MD 20824-0105
(301) 592-8573
nhlbi.nih.gov

National Osteoporosis Foundation
1323 22nd Street NW, Suite 500
Washington, DC 20037-1292
(202) 223-2226
nof.org

National Strength and Conditioning Association
1885 Bob Johnson Drive
Colorado Springs, CO 80906
(888) 815-6826
nsca-lift.org

President's Council on Physical Fitness and Sports
200 Independence Avenue SW
Room 738 H
Washington, DC 20201-0004
(202) 690-9000
fitness.gov

Shape Up America!
15009 Native Dancer Road
North Potomac, MD 20878
(240) 715-3900
shapeup.org

U.S. Department of Agriculture
Center for Nutrition Policy and Promotion
1400 Independence Avenue
Washington, DC 20250
(202) 606-8000
usda.gov

Index

About the Author

Harvey B. Simon, M.D., is an associate professor of medicine at Harvard Medical School and a member of the Health Sciences Technology faculty at Massachusetts Institute of Technology. His commitment to education was recognized when he was awarded the London Prize for Excellence in Teaching by Harvard and MIT.

Dr. Simon is a graduate of Yale College and Harvard Medical School. Since completing his postgraduate training at Massachusetts General Hospital and the National Institutes of Health, he has maintained an active clinical practice at Massachusetts General Hospital.

For the past thirty years, Dr. Simon has had an intense personal and professional commitment to the study and promotion of exercise for health. He is a founding member of the Harvard Cardiovascular Health Center, has served on the Massachusetts Governor's Committee on Physical Fitness and Sports and has been a member of the American College of Sports Medicine. Among his many scientific publications are medical articles and textbook chapters on exercise, nutrition, and sports medicine.

Dr. Simon is the founding editor of the *Harvard Men's Health Watch*. He is the award-winning author of scores of magazine articles and five previous books on health and fitness.

Dr. Simon lives with his wife in the Boston area; they have two daughters and four grandchildren.